Effective DevRel

Learn How to Succeed in the Field of Developer Relations

Kurtis Kemple

Apress®

Effective DevRel: Learn How to Succeed in the Field of Developer Relations

Kurtis Kemple
Chesapeake, VA, USA

ISBN-13 (pbk): 979-8-8688-2372-5 ISBN-13 (electronic): 979-8-8688-2373-2
https://doi.org/10.1007/979-8-8688-2373-2

Managing Director, Apress Media LLC: Welmoed Spahr
Acquisitions Editor: Anandadeep Roy
Editorial Assistant: Jessica Vakili

Cover designed by eStudioCalamar

Distributed to the book trade worldwide by Springer Science+Business Media New York, 1 New York Plaza, New York, NY 10004. Phone 1-800-SPRINGER, fax (201) 348-4505, e-mail orders-ny@springer-sbm.com, or visit www.springeronline.com. Apress Media, LLC is a Delaware LLC and the sole member (owner) is Springer Science + Business Media Finance Inc (SSBM Finance Inc). SSBM Finance Inc is a **Delaware** corporation.

For information on translations, please e-mail booktranslations@springernature.com; for reprint, paperback, or audio rights, please e-mail bookpermissions@springernature.com.

Apress titles may be purchased in bulk for academic, corporate, or promotional use. eBook versions and licenses are also available for most titles. For more information, reference our Print and eBook Bulk Sales web page at http://www.apress.com/bulk-sales.

Any source code or other supplementary material referenced by the author in this book is available to readers on GitHub. For more detailed information, please visit https://www.apress.com/gp/services/source-code.

If disposing of this product, please recycle the paper

To my wife, Donna, and to my children, Dawson and Miles—thank you for your unwavering support and for believing in me even in the moments when I struggled to believe in myself. This book exists because you never let me quit.

Table of Contents

About the Author

Kurtis Kemple is a recognized leader in Developer Relations and platform strategy, known for applying a systems-driven, first-principles approach to complex organizational and technical challenges. He entered the field through an unconventional path, teaching himself to code while incarcerated—an experience that shaped his discipline of learning from fundamentals and his instinct for recognizing the structural forces behind system behavior.

Over the past two decades, he has led developer experience and product strategy at companies including Amazon, Apollo GraphQL, Slack, and Salesforce. His work focuses on identifying friction in developer and organizational workflows, understanding how teams evolve under pressure, and building DevRel programs that translate developer success into measurable business outcomes.

Kurtis is also a writer, speaker, and coach. Through his advisory work at Phi Group, he helps leaders solve complex strategic problems by grounding decisions in evidence, structural analysis, and the real-world behavior of systems nearing their constraints. He is currently pursuing a master's in Physics at the Open University in the UK.

About the Technical Reviewer

Kim Maida is a Developer Relations and Developer Experience leader and strategist, operations engineer, international public speaker, and identity and security practitioner. She enjoys teaching, mentoring, and learning from others in the product technology space. She loves to travel, overland cross-country, design stickers, and craft dioramas, miniatures, and artisan keycaps for mechanical keyboards.

Acknowledgments

Projects like this one are never truly solo, even when most of the work is done in silence with a blank page and a stubborn idea.

I'm deeply grateful to my technical reviewer, Kim Maida, whose thoughtful feedback and careful attention to detail helped sharpen the arguments in this book. A good technical review doesn't just catch mistakes; it forces you to be clearer about what you really mean. Kim did exactly that.

I also want to thank Angie Jones for contributing the foreword. Angie has long been a voice I respect at the intersection of engineering, leadership, and community, and having her frame this book for readers is an honor. Her perspective sets the stage for what follows in a way I could not have done alone.

My thanks as well to the editorial and production team at Apress for guiding the manuscript through the publishing process and turning a collection of pages into a finished book. Their work is mostly invisible to readers, but it is essential to everything you now hold in your hands.

Finally, I'm grateful for the broader developer and DevRel communities that made this book necessary in the first place. The lessons here were forged in real teams, real constraints, and real trade-offs. If anything in these pages proves useful, it's because of the people who showed me, over many years, what effective Developer Relations can look like when it's done with intention.

Introduction

Developer Relations has always suffered from a clarity problem.

Ask ten leaders what DevRel does, and you'll get eleven answers. Some describe it as community-building. Others call it top-of-funnel marketing. Some treat it as support with better storytelling. A few still imagine it as a kind of technical evangelism whose job is to "get developers excited." None of these are entirely wrong, but none describe the full picture either.

The truth is simpler and more demanding: **Developer Relations is the function responsible for connecting developer success to business outcomes.** Everything else—content, community, advocacy, education, tooling—is simply how that connection takes shape.

Yet despite DevRel's increasing importance, the role remains unevenly understood inside many organizations. Teams try to demonstrate value by doing more rather than understanding what matters. Activity substitutes for impact. Road maps stretch wider without getting deeper. And as the industry changes, many DevRel functions find themselves reacting to shifts they should have anticipated.

This book exists to create clarity where the field still has ambiguity.

It distills nearly a decade of practical experience at developer-first and developer-plus companies, years of observing where DevRel succeeds and where it collapses, and hundreds of patterns gathered from practitioners around the world. It is not a collection of tactics. It is a system—one that treats DevRel as a strategic function whose purpose is measurable, repeatable, and core to a company's success.

You'll see that system unfold across the chapters ahead.

Chapter 1 lays the foundation by answering the question that quietly sits underneath almost every conversation about this field: what DevRel actually does and why it matters. It introduces the Developer Relations Value Cycle—engagement, impact, and enablement—and shows how these components, when working together, turn DevRel into a genuine force multiplier for both developers and the business. Chapter 2 turns the lens inward and grounds the work in an organizational context. DevRel cannot be effective without understanding the nature of the company it sits within—whether it is developer-first or developer-plus, how it goes to market, what its growth stage demands, and where DevRel sits structurally. These elements shape the expectations and constraints the function must navigate.

From there, Chapter 3 shifts to the developer's perspective. Instead of relying on the linear funnels that have become industry shorthand, it explores the far more realistic journey developers actually take: nonlinear, cyclical, contextual, and deeply influenced by the environments they work within. Mapping these journeys with precision exposes friction that would otherwise go unnoticed and reveals opportunities that can fundamentally change the trajectory of a platform.

The chapters that follow deepen this system in practical ways. You'll move from understanding developer journeys to turning their experiences into actionable insight—using structured audits, friction logs, and evidence-based reporting to influence product decisions with clarity and credibility. You'll explore what it means to evolve from an individual contributor into a strategic leader, building systems rather than activities and becoming a partner to the business rather than a reactive executor. You'll learn how to escape the gravitational pull of "random acts of DevRel" by putting in place operational frameworks that scale impact without scaling burnout.

Finally, the book looks ahead. It shows how the most effective DevRel leaders operate across multiple time horizons, filter signal from noise, and anticipate shifts before they become industry narratives. The appendixes offer the practical scaffolding that brings these ideas to life—models, frameworks, and tools designed for real use in complex environments.

Together, these components form a coherent approach to DevRel: one that replaces ambiguity with structure, and activity with intentional, measurable value.

You don't need to adopt every model and process shared in this book to benefit from it. What matters is learning to think systemically about DevRel—about how developer needs intersect with business objectives, how insight becomes action, and how the function becomes indispensable when it focuses on the right work.

If you've ever struggled to explain DevRel's purpose, or felt caught in a cycle of producing outputs without seeing meaningful outcomes, or sensed industry shifts approaching before your organization did, this book is for you.

What follows is not just a handbook for executing DevRel well. It's a blueprint for building DevRel into a strategic asset—one capable of improving developer experience, shaping product direction, and strengthening the businesses that depend on developers to succeed.

PART I

Positioning for Success

CHAPTER 1

The Value of DevRel

"What exactly does Developer Relations do anyway?" It's a question I've faced countless times throughout my career, and judging by conversations with peers across the industry, I'm not alone. The reality is that our work often occurs at the intersections between developers and products, between communities and companies, and between technical needs and business goals. This intersection work is inherently difficult to quantify, but that doesn't make it any less valuable.

Why DevRel Matters: Connecting Developers to Business Outcomes

Developer Relations sits at this weird, messy junction in tech companies. While most teams are looking either entirely inward or outward, we're constantly swiveling our heads in both directions. We're translating developer needs to the company while trying to make the company's capabilities make sense to developers. It's exhausting but incredibly powerful when done right.

Here's the thing about effective DevRel—it creates this magic connection between developer success and business outcomes. When developers can actually use your stuff to build cool things, they're demonstrating your platform's value better than any marketing campaign ever could. As more developers build successfully, your platform grows in usage, reputation, and, yes, revenue. This isn't just feel-good work; it's strategic business growth.

Note At Apollo GraphQL, developer feedback kept highlighting the same friction point—developers couldn't easily try our GraphQL API inspection tool (GraphOS Explorer) without creating an account first. The pattern was clear in our data—people would get excited about the Explorer, hit the account wall, and bounce.

K. Kemple, *Effective DevRel*, https://doi.org/10.1007/979-8-8688-2373-2_1

Instead of just documenting this problem, our DevRel team gathered qualitative feedback from developers and journey audits, as well as quantitative data about Explorer usage patterns.

Armed with this evidence, we convinced the Product team to expose the tool through a web IDE without requiring a sign-up. The results shocked everyone—20,000 new sign-ups in the first month alone, with consistent growth afterward. We didn't build anything new; we just removed a barrier that our conversations with developers identified and journey audits and data confirmed. That's the DevRel magic—translating developer friction into business growth.

In today's tech landscape, companies that engage developers well gain serious advantages:

- Developers adopt your new features way faster.
- Your platform becomes stickier as it embeds in developer workflows.
- Happy developers tell other developers about you (the best marketing ever).
- You get brutally honest product feedback from people using your stuff.
- Your support costs drop because developers can help themselves.

These advantages snowball over time. They're not just quarterly wins; they're sustainable business value that compounds year after year.

The Evolution and Purpose of Developer Relations

DevRel wasn't always a thing, you know? It emerged when companies realized that developers need different approaches than traditional buyers. As technical platforms got increasingly complex and developers started influencing purchasing decisions more, conventional marketing wasn't cutting it.

The first wave of DevRel was mostly about awareness and technical evangelism—basically explaining complicated tech and promoting adoption through conference talks, meetups, and basic content. It was necessary groundwork but often disconnected from actual business metrics.

As the field matured, DevRel expanded beyond just evangelism. We started owning documentation, SDKs, developer feedback, technical support, and education. This expansion happened because smart companies realized successful developer platforms needed more than awareness; they required comprehensive support throughout the entire developer journey.

Today's DevRel has evolved into something more strategic. Modern DevRel professionals don't just create awareness; we drive adoption, retention, and expansion through sophisticated programs that address the complete developer experience. We've gone from "Hey, check out this cool tech" to "Let's make sure you're successful at every step."

The fundamental purpose hasn't changed, though—we're here to help developers succeed with our technology while ensuring our companies understand and address what developers actually need. This dual mandate makes us different from other functions and forms the heart of our unique value.

Beyond Awareness: The Developer Relations Value Cycle

At its core, DevRel's value comes from being the only function that can authentically represent developer and business perspectives. We create a powerful feedback loop of engagement, impact, and enablement that I call the Developer Relations Value Cycle (DRVC).

The DRVC is similar to other frameworks like Mary Thengvall's "DevRel Path to Success," with one key difference: "awareness" is replaced with "impact." This shift acknowledges two critical realities of modern DevRel work:

1. DevRel functions as a force multiplier—internally and externally—and traditional models often underrepresent our internal impact.

2. Awareness is typically a marketing responsibility, while DevRel teams frequently work horizontally across organizations (similar to growth teams) or align with product or engineering. Using "impact" provides flexibility that better reflects the diversity of DevRel responsibilities in today's industry.

Note It's worth highlighting that the earlier frameworks really did the job for DevRel's "first wave." They set us up with the basics—spreading awareness, technical evangelism, and getting those first communities going. Acknowledging the achievements of those before us shows how today's efforts are all about building on that solid foundation. As DevRel has grown, so have our goals and challenges, and the Developer Relations Value Cycle reflects that expanded scope, bringing new dimensions to the work established in those early days.

Let's break down each component of the cycle.

Engagement: The Foundation of Context

Engagement is the foundation of developer relations, but not simply for the sake of being active in communities. **The person who gains the most value from engagement is you.**

As developer relations professionals, we can do something neither a company nor a community can do alone: exist meaningfully in each world. The genuine value of DevRel is the context you gain by deeply understanding the needs, frustrations, and aspirations of developers and companies. The deeper we embed ourselves in each world, the more context we gain, becoming more effective advocates for each side of the relationship.

This focus on context separates the value of DevRel from any individual personality. Your context can be

- Passed on to others
- Combined with context from team members
- Systematized into organizational knowledge

This perspective also helps reduce the stigma that you need an established community presence to become a DevRel professional, making the field more accessible to newcomers with diverse backgrounds and experiences.

Build relationships to build context. This mantra captures the essence of engagement in the DRVC.

Impact: Translating Context into Organizational Value

Impact represents the value you bring to your company by providing context to internal teams. Rather than measuring success by the number of talks given or articles published, impact focuses on how your work influences business outcomes and product decisions.

Examples of impact include

- Helping marketing and sales teams develop more authentic, technically accurate messaging and content
- Providing feedback and insights to product and engineering teams based on developer needs
- Driving cross-functional initiatives that increase platform adoption
- Advocating for changes to pricing, features, or policies based on developer feedback

Where DevRel sits within the organization largely determines who you impact and what metrics will matter most. Let's examine how organizational structure influences DevRel's focus and impact.

When DevRel Sits Within Marketing

In this structure, DevRel typically focuses on top-of-funnel metrics and qualified leads. Your work will likely be predominantly outbound, including creating content, building example projects, speaking at events, and networking with developers. You'll likely also be responsible for managing developer relationships.

When DevRel Sits Within Product/Engineering

Here, goals typically center on driving product adoption and providing product feedback and business insights. While your work remains predominately outbound, you'll likely engage in more one-on-one developer interactions to understand how people use the products you support.

If Developer Experience (DevXP) is within DevRel, you'll also oversee tooling, SDKs, and other developer enablement projects, such as sample applications.

When DevRel Operates As a Standalone Function

In this organizational structure, DevRel exists outside the traditional functions of Marketing or Product. Goals and metrics become less predefined in this model. Here, DevRel operates most like a Growth team. You'll need to identify and fill gaps in responsibility along key developer journeys. Success depends on building relationships and leveraging cross-functional collaboration to drive meaningful impact.

Enablement: Closing the Loop

Enablement is the value you bring to developers by removing friction from their workflows, creating resources that fill information gaps, supporting developers through connection and opportunity, and recognizing their contributions.

The most significant impact DevRel can have is removing friction from developers' workflows. This approach has the dual benefit of improving business metrics while providing tangible value to developers:

- Improving onboarding reduces churn and makes it easier for developers to use a service they need.
- Providing feedback on an API improves MAUs and simplifies developers' work with your platform.
- Advocating for consumption-based pricing can improve Net Revenue Retention (NRR) and plan expansion, increase MAU by opening features to more developers, provide compelling marketing campaigns, and help developers by making more of the platform accessible.

As DevRel professionals, we can walk through entire developer workflows—from concept to value creation—and document our experiences, applying context from company and community perspectives. This process allows us to identify friction that might otherwise remain invisible (what I call "product opportunities") and provide actionable steps to remove it.

Enablement forms the foundation for building lasting relationships with developers. They will come to rely on you, confide in you, and often advocate for you because they know you're invested in their success. However, they won't provide valuable feedback if they don't believe you advocate for changes that benefit them or invest in their growth.

Developer Experience As a Competitive Advantage

Let me tell you something that might be uncomfortable to hear—in today's world, superior technology alone just isn't enough anymore. Developers have so many options now, and their experiences with your platform dramatically influence whether they adopt, stick around, or tell others about you. The companies winning big are the ones recognizing that developer experience isn't nice to have; it's a serious competitive advantage.

Developer experience covers every single interaction developers have with you—from that first curious Google search through implementation and ongoing usage. It's your docs (are they clear or a mess?), your API design (intuitive or head-scratching?), your SDKs (helpful or hindrance?), your onboarding (smooth or painful?), your support (responsive or crickets?), and countless other touchpoints. All these experiences add up to determine whether developers merely tolerate your platform or become genuine advocates who tell everyone about you.

Good DevRel programs directly improve this experience by

- Finding and fixing those friction points that slow developers down
- Creating learning materials that don't assume everyone's an expert
- Building bridges between what's technically possible and practically implementable
- Fighting for developer-friendly product changes from the inside
- Providing clear paths from "What is this thing?" to "Look what I built!"

When companies nail developer experience, they see real business benefits:

- Developers get to value faster, increasing activation rates.
- Support costs drop because people can actually figure things out themselves.
- Your platform becomes harder to rip out once it's integrated into workflows.
- Word-of-mouth explodes as developers share positive experiences.
- Competitors find it harder to steal your developers away.

This connection between developer experience and business results transforms DevRel from a nice marketing addition into a strategic investment with measurable returns. By systematically making life better for developers using your platform, you create competitive advantages that fancy features alone just can't match.

DEVREL MATURITY ASSESSMENT

Let's take stock of where you are today. Grab a pen—seriously, do this right now! Rate your DevRel program from 1 (we're just figuring this out) to 5 (we've totally nailed this) in each area:

1. Score your engagement strength

   __ How present are you in the communities where your developers hang out?

   __ Are you systematically collecting and documenting feedback?

   __ Have you built relationships with key developers who influence others?

   __ Do you have a process for sharing what you learn with the rest of your company?

2. Score your internal impact

   __ Is your work clearly aligned with what the business actually cares about?

   __ Can you point to product decisions you've influenced?

   __ Are you measurably contributing to adoption and retention?

   __ Have you built strong relationships across different teams?

3. Score your developer enablement

   __ How comprehensive are your learning resources?
   __ Is your onboarding experience smooth?
   __ Are you regularly creating content that helps developers succeed?
   __ Do you recognize and reward developers who contribute?

Now for the hard part...

Add up your scores in each category (each has a maximum of 20 points). Be honest—which area is your weakest? Draft a simple action plan that focuses on your lowest scores first.

If you scored below 12 in any category, that's your red flag; start there!

You'll get the most bang for your buck bringing up your weakest area, rather than polishing what's already working well.

Conclusion: Breaking the Random Acts of DevRel Cycle

Without a clear value framework, DevRel teams often fall into the trap of "random acts of DevRel"—disconnected activities that might generate content or community engagement but fail to create sustainable value for developers or the business. The Developer Relations Value Cycle provides a structure for intentional, strategic DevRel work.

By focusing on the interdependent relationship between engagement, impact, and enablement, we can transform DevRel from a difficult-to-quantify function into a strategic asset that demonstrably drives developer success and business outcomes.

Regardless of the specific framework you choose to represent the value of developer relations, develop a few key questions that describe the outcomes of your actions rather than just listing activities. This approach will help you focus on what matters and communicate your value more effectively to organizational stakeholders.

CHAPTER 2

Navigating Your Organizational Context

If Chapter 1 establishes what DevRel does, this chapter focuses on the context in which DevRel operates. Too often, DevRel teams operate in isolation from business realities, leading to misaligned goals, wasted resources, and diminished impact. By understanding your company's business model, growth stage, and organizational structure, you can create DevRel strategies that amplify business goals while still genuinely serving developer needs.

Note I watched a DevRel team disappear once. They had spent months making these videos about their product, putting in late hours to get everything perfect. The problem was that their product was still finding product-market fit and changing constantly. By the time they published anything, it was quickly going to become outdated. Developers got frustrated, leadership couldn't see any value, and when money got tight… the entire team was let go just like that. All those talented people were gone because their work wasn't aligned with what the company really needed. A harsh reminder that technical skill alone isn't enough without understanding your organizational context.

Developer-First vs. Developer+ Business Models

When approaching Developer Relations, you need to understand the fundamental role developers play in your company's success. This understanding shapes everything from your communication style to your strategic priorities.

Developer-oriented companies typically fall into two distinct categories, each requiring a different DevRel approach.

K. Kemple, *Effective DevRel*, https://doi.org/10.1007/979-8-8688-2373-2_2

Developer-First Companies

These are businesses where developers are the primary decision-makers and users. Examples include GitHub, Netlify, MongoDB, and other tools and platforms primarily used by developer audiences. In these companies

- Developers are both users and buyers
- Product decisions prioritize developer experience
- Marketing speaks directly to technical audiences

This model shapes everything from messaging to product road maps. When developers control both usage and purchasing decisions, their technical preferences become the primary consideration for the entire business.

Developer+ Companies

These businesses serve developers and target stakeholders like business users, data scientists, marketers, or operations teams. Examples include Slack, Twilio, and other platforms where developers build for broader organizational needs. In these companies

- Developers are users but rarely the sole decision-makers
- Multiple personas influence the buying process
- Product decisions prioritize user experience
- Marketing and messaging must bridge technical and business value
- They generally use a marketing and sales funnel GTM strategy

Developer+ companies face the challenge of satisfying both technical requirements and business objectives. Their products must work technically *and* deliver business outcomes that justify investment.

Understanding which model your company follows is crucial because it fundamentally shapes how DevRel should operate. In a developer-first company, you focus heavily on technical depth and feature adoption. In a developer-plus company, DevRel must also help translate between technical and business value, showing how developer solutions address broader organizational needs.

Company Growth Stages and Their Impact on DevRel

Your company's growth stage determines available resources, priorities, and the most effective DevRel approaches. A startup with three engineers has vastly different DevRel needs than an enterprise with thousands of customers. Let's look at how different growth stages impact DevRel strategies and execution.

Startup Stage Impact on DevRel

Startups represent the earliest and most dynamic phase of a company's lifecycle. These organizations are in an experimental phase, working to validate their product-market fit while building their initial user base. With everything still in flux, startups must be incredibly adaptable and responsive to market feedback.

Companies at this stage typically

- Have limited resources and small, agile teams
- Iterate rapidly based on market feedback
- Follow a product-led growth (PLG) approach
- Make quick decisions with minimal bureaucracy

Impact on DevRel: In startups, DevRel often means wearing multiple hats and focusing on foundations. You might be the entire "team"—handling documentation, creating initial content, gathering feedback, and representing developers internally. Your priority should be helping the product find its fit with developers while establishing credible technical communication. You'll need to be highly versatile, comfortable with ambiguity, and focused on quick wins that demonstrate value.

Scale-Up Stage Impact on DevRel

Scale-ups have successfully navigated the startup phase and are entering a period of significant growth. Having proven their market fit and secured substantial funding, these companies face the exciting but challenging task of transitioning from a scrappy startup to a more structured organization while maintaining their innovative spirit.

These companies generally

- Experience rapid team expansion
- Establish formal processes and structures
- Balance growth with maintaining existing quality
- Add a marketing/sales funnel to their go-to-market (GTM) strategy
- Seek to acquire their first enterprise customers

Impact on DevRel: DevRel in scale-ups often expands from one generalist to a small, specialized team. The challenges shift from establishing basics to creating systems that can scale with the company. Your focus should be on building proper documentation, creating repeatable developer onboarding processes, and establishing feedback mechanisms between developers and the product team. This stage requires you to balance maintaining what works while building for future growth.

Enterprise Stage Impact on DevRel

Enterprise companies have achieved significant market presence and operational maturity. These organizations have successfully scaled their operations and now face the unique challenges of maintaining their market position while continuing to expand their enterprise customer base.

At this stage, organizations typically

- Maintain a multiproduct portfolio
- Manage complex organizational structures
- Serve multiple stakeholder groups
- Balance innovation with maintaining existing offerings
- Follow sophisticated business processes
- Incorporate enterprise features like SSO, security certifications, and compliance standards

Impact on DevRel: In enterprises, DevRel often comprises specialized teams with defined responsibilities. Your challenges include ensuring consistency across products, scaling impact through systems rather than individual heroics, and aligning with complex organizational priorities. You'll need to navigate established processes while maintaining the developer-centric authenticity that makes DevRel valuable. Cross-team coordination becomes crucial as you work with dedicated documentation, marketing, and support functions.

Aligning DevRel with Go-to-Market Approaches

DevRel strategies must align with your company's marketing approach. Understanding whether your company follows a product-led growth model or a traditional marketing/sales pipeline helps you position DevRel initiatives effectively and measure success appropriately.

Product-Led Growth Alignment

In PLG companies, the product itself drives user acquisition, conversion, and expansion. The PLG model typically includes stages like

- **Evaluate:** Developers discover and assess your product.
- **Activate:** Developers achieve initial success with your product.
- **Adopt:** Developers integrate your product into their workflows.
- **Expand:** Developers increase usage and explore new capabilities.
- **Advocate:** Satisfied developers recommend your product to others.

DevRel Alignment with PLG: When your company follows a PLG approach, your DevRel activities should support this flywheel. Focus your efforts on

- Creating evaluation content that helps developers assess product fit
- Building activation resources that accelerate time-to-first success
- Developing adoption guides that showcase integration patterns
- Highlighting advanced use cases that encourage expansion
- Nurturing and amplifying product advocates

The PLG model demands extreme focus on removing friction from the developer journey, as each point of resistance can interrupt the flywheel's momentum. Your metrics should track progression through these flywheel stages rather than traditional marketing funnel metrics.

Marketing/Sales Pipeline Alignment

Companies using traditional go-to-market approaches typically use a funnel to track customer journey stages. A marketing funnel typically includes stages like

- **Awareness:** Developers discover your product exists.
- **Acquisition:** Developers visit your site or sign up for information.
- **Activation:** Developers experience initial value from your product.
- **Retention:** Developers return to use your product repeatedly.
- **Revenue:** Developers convert to paying customers or expand usage.
- **Referral:** Developers recommend your product to others.

DevRel Alignment with Pipeline

When your company follows a pipeline approach, align your activities to support different funnel stages:

- **Awareness:** Create technical blog posts and speak at conferences to drive awareness.
- **Acquisition:** Develop technical tutorials and interactive demos to encourage sign-ups.
- **Activation:** Build quick-start guides and first-project templates to accelerate activation.
- **Retention:** Develop comprehensive documentation and use-case examples to support retention.
- **Revenue:** Provide technical enablement through workshops and webinars to support conversion.
- **Referral:** Cultivate advocates through recognition programs to drive referrals.

Many common DevRel tactics work in both models but need to be framed differently. By understanding your company's approach, you can present your work using terminology and metrics that resonate with stakeholders while still delivering authentic, helpful resources to developers.

Where DevRel Sits in the Organization and Why It Matters

DevRel's organizational home significantly impacts its focus, resources, and cross-functional relationships. Where your function reports directly shape your team's priorities and how success is measured.

Marketing Placement Impact

When DevRel reports to Marketing leadership, it usually focuses on

- Awareness and top-of-funnel metrics
- Content creation and distribution
- Event presence and developer outreach
- Growth and engagement

Why This Matters

This placement gives you clear alignment with awareness and acquisition goals, natural collaboration with content and events teams, and typically better resources for outreach activities. You'll have strong support for activities that generate visibility and initial developer interest.

However, you might struggle to influence product decisions, feel pressure to prioritize quantity over quality, and sometimes face tension between authentic developer relationships and marketing objectives. Maintaining technical depth and credibility can require deliberate effort in this organizational structure.

Product/Engineering Placement Impact

When DevRel reports to Product or Engineering leadership, it typically emphasizes

- Product feedback and feature adoption
- Technical content and documentation
- Developer experience and friction reduction
- Development of developer tools (CLIs, SDKs, etc.)

Why This Matters

This placement gives you stronger influence on product decisions, typically deeper technical focus, and natural alignment with engineering workflows. You'll likely have more impact on the product itself and a stronger voice in technical decisions.

The challenges include limited marketing resources, difficulty with awareness initiatives, and sometimes tension between product timelines and developer needs. Getting resources for top-of-funnel activities can be an uphill battle when reporting to Product or Engineering.

Standalone Function Impact

When DevRel operates as an independent function reporting directly to executive leadership, it typically

- Takes a more balanced approach across the developer journey
- Has greater flexibility to decide on priorities
- Works horizontally across multiple parts of the organization

Why This Matters

This placement gives you more autonomy, potential for broader impact, and the ability to define balanced success metrics. You can create a more comprehensive developer experience without inherent biases toward marketing or product priorities.

The challenges include the potential lack of clear executive sponsorship, the need to build multiple cross-functional relationships, and more vigorous internal advocacy for resources. Without a natural "home," you'll need to work harder to establish clear value propositions for different stakeholders.

It's also worth noting that placing DevRel under the C-suite adds direct responsibility to executive leadership, a setup that's relatively uncommon—particularly in scale-ups and enterprises that are cautious about expanding direct reports at the highest level.

Hybrid Structure Impact

Increasingly, companies are adopting hybrid models where DevRel responsibilities are distributed across the organization:

- Developer Marketing sits within Marketing.
- Developer Advocacy sits within Product.
- Developer Experience sits within Engineering.

Why This Matters

This structure aligns specialized functions with their natural organizational homes, potentially improving efficiency and focus for each team. However, it requires exceptional coordination to present a unified developer experience externally. Without strong communication channels and aligned goals, developers may encounter inconsistent experiences as they interact with different parts of your organization.

Understanding your organizational placement helps you lean into its advantages while proactively addressing its limitations. No structure is perfect, and successful DevRel leaders adapt their strategies to work effectively within their specific organizational context.

DOCUMENTING YOUR ORGANIZATIONAL CONTEXT

Take time to analyze your organization's business context by answering these key questions:

1. Identify your company's primary model: Is it developer-first or developer+? What specific evidence supports this classification?
2. Determine your company's growth stage (startup, scale-up, or enterprise). What are the three primary challenges your DevRel team faces at this stage?
3. List your company's top three to five growth metrics. For each metric, identify at least one way DevRel can directly influence it.
4. Document where DevRel sits in your organization. List three specific advantages and three limitations of this placement.

5. Determine if your company is primarily PLG or pipeline-driven. Identify how this approach influences your content strategy and success metrics.

6. Map your five most important stakeholders across the organization. For each, note their primary goals and how DevRel supports them.

7. Identify three potential gaps in cross-functional collaboration. For each gap, suggest a practical approach to improve alignment.

Create a one-page summary of your organizational context that you can reference when planning DevRel initiatives.

Conclusion: Why Organizational Context Matters

Successful DevRel requires a deep understanding of business strategy and organizational dynamics. Whether at a startup or an enterprise, every initiative you launch should connect developer needs with company objectives.

DevRel teams that operate in isolation eventually become irrelevant or expendable. Those that deeply integrate with business priorities become essential strategic partners. By understanding your company's business model, growth stage, organizational structure, and go-to-market approach, you position your DevRel function for sustainable impact.

Remember, your effectiveness as a DevRel professional depends on your ability to navigate your unique business environment while staying true to developer needs. Use what you've learned here to position your initiatives in ways that resonate with both developers and business leaders.

This organizational context serves as the foundation for everything else we'll explore in this book. With this understanding, you can create DevRel strategies that drive meaningful value rather than just generate activity.

CHAPTER 3

Mapping the Developer Journey

While understanding your business context is essential, gaining deep insight into how developers experience your platform is even more important. Developer journeys are rarely straightforward or predictable. They're nonlinear and generally highly individualized.

This chapter moves from the company's perspective to the developer's experience. By mapping the developer journey with precision and empathy, we can identify the critical moments where DevRel initiatives can remove friction, accelerate adoption, and transform casual users into passionate advocates.

Why Traditional Journey Maps Fail DevRel Teams

The traditional view of customer or developer journeys often presents a linear path from awareness to adoption. But developers rarely follow such straightforward routes. Their journeys are typically:

- **Nonlinear**: Moving back and forth between stages as they explore, evaluate, and experiment
- **Cyclical**: Revisiting earlier stages as they expand usage or reassess decisions
- **Contextual**: Heavily influenced by their specific technical environment, team dynamics, and organizational constraints
- **Experience-driven**: Shaped by the cumulative effect of multiple interactions, not just a single touchpoint

K. Kemple, *Effective DevRel*, https://doi.org/10.1007/979-8-8688-2373-2_3

Traditional journey maps also often fail because they rely on idealized, sequential progressions that don't match real developer behavior.

They tend to

- Present a single path when developers take many different routes
- Focus on company touchpoints rather than developer needs
- Neglect the critical influence of existing technical environments
- Overlook the iterative nature of technical adoption
- Ignore the social dynamics of technical decision-making
- Tie touchpoints to specific stages of the journey

Understanding this complexity is crucial for effective DevRel. Rather than forcing developers through a predefined path, we need to meet them where they are and support their natural decision-making processes.

Touchpoints vs. Milestones: The Critical Distinction

To map developer journeys effectively, we need to distinguish between two types of interactions. This distinction is at the heart of understanding how developers actually progress with your technology rather than how we wish they would. When we blur these two concepts together, we end up measuring activity instead of meaningful progress, and that's where so many DevRel teams go wrong.

Touchpoints

Touchpoints are discrete moments of interaction between developers and your company. These include

- Reading a blog post or documentation page
- Watching a tutorial video
- Attending a webinar or conference talk
- Downloading an SDK or sample app
- Asking a question in a forum
- Interacting with support

These touchpoints are essential, but they don't tell the whole story. A developer might interact with dozens of touchpoints without making meaningful progress toward adoption.

Milestones

Milestones are the critical moments where multiple touchpoints culminate in a significant shift in the developer's relationship with your product. These include

- Creating their first working application
- Deploying to production
- Successfully integrating with their existing stack
- Demonstrating value to stakeholders
- Making a purchase decision
- Expanding usage to new use cases

These milestones move developers forward in their journey. They are the moments that matter most for adoption and growth.

Traditional journey maps often focus exclusively on touchpoints, tracking every interaction without distinguishing which ones actually drive progress. By focusing on milestones, you shift from measuring activity to measuring meaningful progress.

Note To put this into perspective, at Slack, we measured app creation, app installs to workspaces, and another metric called "**Meaningful Usage**," which equates to an app reaching three user days in a seven-day period (*i.e., the app was used three times within a week by either the same person three different days or three different people on any day*) as the milestones we could impact the most.

These have tangible value for the business (*more on how we were able to connect those dots in Chapter 10)* and were measures that DevRel could directly affect. With these milestones mapped, we could then measure things like time-to-value and conversion rate from milestone to milestone, providing us with clear metrics to focus our initiatives on.

Key Milestones and Touchpoints Across the Developer Journey

Let me break down what the developer journey looks like—not the idealized version, but the reality of how developers progress. Each phase has a critical milestone with touchpoints that either help developers advance or leave them struggling. I've spent years watching these patterns repeat, and trust me, they're remarkably consistent across different platforms and developer types.

Discovery → First Meaningful Interaction

Developers first notice your platform and decide whether to invest their time. That moment when they think, "Okay, this might be worth digging into," is gold; it's the difference between a bounce and the start of a relationship. Important touchpoints include

- Search results that match their intent
- Technical content that shows an understanding of their problem
- Social proof from other developers they trust
- Evaluative documentation that acknowledges limitations

The goal should be to drive down clicks-to-action for developers evaluating your platform. To do that, you need to understand what touchpoints help developers get to that first meaningful interaction within your developer journey.

First Meaningful Interaction → First Working Application

This is where theory and exploration meet practice. The moment they get something—anything—working is transformative; it converts your platform from a concept to a tool in their toolkit. Developers need

- Tutorials and guides that answer their specific questions
- Code examples they can adapt to their situation
- Troubleshooting guides for common errors

- Tools that reduce time spent on anything other than business logic
- Testing best practices

This is often where DevRel can have the most impact. Getting developers through activation is often where we can have the most success. It's why you'll often see investment in enablement initiatives like tutorials or other types of instructional content, workshops, video series, hackathons, etc., across all DevRel teams. They're foundational to driving adoption by providing immediate relief to developer friction experienced along the journey through direct access to subject matter experts (that's you!).

First Working Application → Production Deployment

The jump from localhost to production is where developers who were confidently experimenting suddenly start asking different questions: How do I handle secrets? What about rate limits? How do I know if something breaks? This shift from "it works on my machine" to "it needs to work for everyone, all the time" fundamentally changes how developers think about your platform.

Developers at this milestone often need

- Environment-specific deployment guides and supporting tooling
- Security checklists and best practices
- Performance optimization best practices
- Monitoring and reliability best practices

Supporting developers through this transition determines whether they become long-term production users or keep your platform in the experimental category, and once that decision is made, it rarely changes without significant effort on both sides.

Production Deployment → Sustainable Operation

The often-overlooked phase where developers spend most of their time. Despite being the longest phase of the relationship, it's frequently the most neglected in terms of support resources and touchpoints. Critical touchpoints include

- Upgrade and migration guides
- Troubleshooting resources

- Monitoring best practices
- Lifecycle management strategies
- Administration tooling and dashboards

This maintenance phase directly impacts your retention metrics and expansion revenue—developers who feel supported through upgrades and changes become long-term customers, while those who hit breaking changes without warning start evaluating competitors and rarely come back once they've invested effort in migration.

Sustainable Operation → Feature Expansion

When expanding across your platform, developers need guidance to venture beyond their comfort zone. This milestone marks the deepening of their investment and often correlates with measures like customer satisfaction and retention. Developers need

- Integration patterns connecting features
- Migration paths for expanding usage
- Feature-specific documentation
- Use cases that demonstrate practical value

This expansion phase is where your platform transforms from a tool they use into a foundation they build upon—and that shift changes everything about how they see your technology and their relationship with it.

When you map these touchpoints to milestones, gaps become apparent. These gaps represent opportunities to focus your DevRel efforts where they'll have the most impact.

Note I've seen teams completely transform their effectiveness by identifying just one or two critical gaps and filling them. DevRel teams that operate like Growth teams—taking ownership of gaps in the user journey where no owner exists and working closely with owners where they do exist—are the ones most likely to find consistent opportunity and drive meaningful impact, especially if they identify gaps directly connected to critical milestones in the journey, which we'll discuss in the next chapter.

This is one of the reasons you see Growth teams advocate for pricing adjustments, free trials, free tiers, etc. Purchasing is a very critical milestone in the user journey.

Once you understand these journey patterns, you need to recognize that not all developers navigate the journey the same way. That's where developer personas come in.

Understanding Developer Personas and Motivations

Developers aren't a monolithic group. Their roles, experience levels, organizational contexts, and individual motivations shape their journeys. Creating developer personas helps you understand these variations and tailor your DevRel strategies accordingly.

Common Developer Personas

While your specific personas will depend on your platform, some developer personas include

- **The First Adopter**: Often the first to evaluate new technologies, focused on innovation and potential, willing to work through rough edges if value appears high.
- **The Implementer**: Tasked with building solutions after initial decisions, focused on reliability and productivity. Often looking for specific use case-based enablement material.
- **The Maintainer**: Responsible for ongoing operations, focused on stability, security, and efficiency.
- **The Architect**: Evaluates strategic fit within larger systems, focused on integration, governance, and long-term viability.
- **The Beginner**: Building skills and experience, focused on learning opportunities and clear explanations.

Each persona has distinct needs, concerns, and evaluation criteria. Effective DevRel meets each persona where they are, addressing their specific questions and challenges.

Motivational Factors

Beyond roles, understanding what motivates different developers helps you create more compelling resources and experiences:

- **Problem-focused**: Seeking specific solutions to immediate challenges, valuing direct applicability
- **Career-focused**: Building skills and experience to advance professionally, valuing opportunities to showcase skill set
- **Efficiency-focused**: Looking to automate or streamline existing processes, valuing time savings
- **Innovation-focused**: Exploring new capabilities and approaches, valuing the art of the possible
- **Stability-focused**: Prioritizing reliability and maintainability, valuing proven solutions

By mapping both personas and motivations, you create a multidimensional understanding of your developer audience that informs content, programs, and engagement strategies.

The Connected Journey

Developers never use your platform in isolation. Their journey is always connected to

- Their existing technology investments and skills
- Organizational processes and approval requirements
- Team dynamics and collaborative workflows
- External pressures like deadlines and business objectives

When you recognize these connections, you can create more valuable resources:

- Integration guides for common technology stacks
- Adoption approaches that account for organizational realities
- Resources designed for teams, not just individual developers
- Tools that help developers demonstrate business value

This broader perspective transforms how you support developers. Instead of focusing solely on your platform, you help them navigate the entire landscape of challenges they face. That's when DevRel truly becomes a strategic partner in developer success.

Now that you understand the concepts, let's get into the messy reality of actually mapping these journeys. *Because theory is great, but the real insights come when you roll up your sleeves and start documenting what developers do vs. what you think they do.*

Journey Mapping in Practice

Journey mapping is more than an academic exercise; it's a practical tool that transforms how you understand and support developers. When done effectively, it reveals the hidden patterns, unexpected detours, and critical moments that shape developer success. Let's explore how to turn journey mapping from theory into actionable insights that drive your DevRel strategy.

Mapping Your Critical Path

The critical path is the sequence of milestones that leads to successful adoption and advocacy (*and should also lead to clear value for the business*). It represents the essential journey your developers need to complete to become successful with your platform.

To identify your critical path

1. **Start at the end**: Define what successful adoption looks like for your platform. Is it a production deployment? Regular active usage? Paid conversion?

2. **Work backward**: What milestones must a developer pass through to reach that success state? What dependencies exist between these points?

3. **Identify the minimum path**: What's the shortest viable path to success? This becomes your critical path. Your "make the right thing easy," if you will.

4. **Map the supporting touchpoints**: What interactions support each milestone on the critical path?

By mapping this critical path, you create a strategic framework for DevRel initiatives. Allocate resources based on how effectively they support developers in reaching the next milestone on the critical path.

For example, if deploying a first application is a critical milestone, you might prioritize the following:

- Sample applications that can be deployed with minimal modification
- Clear deployment guides for common environments
- Troubleshooting resources for common deployment issues
- Success validation tools that confirm proper setup (like CLI doctor commands)

This approach ensures you're investing in resources that directly support the most important milestones in the developer journey.

Practical Journey Mapping Approach

By examining real developer experiences rather than idealized paths, you'll discover opportunities to remove friction, accelerate adoption, and create more meaningful developer engagements. This practical approach ensures your DevRel initiatives address actual developer needs rather than assumed ones.

1. **Gather data from multiple sources**
    a. Direct conversations with developers across different stages and personas
    b. Analytics that reveal actual usage patterns, not just what we hope happens
    c. Support tickets and survey results that highlight where developers get stuck
    d. Insights from sales and customer success teams who hear unfiltered feedback

2. **Create visual journey maps that reflect reality**
    a. Map both everyday touchpoints and significant milestones
    b. Document sentiment at each stage: satisfaction, confusion, frustration
    c. Capture the specific questions developers ask at critical moments
    d. Identify gaps where support is missing or insufficient
3. **Validate with developers who use your platform**
    a. Share your journey maps with actual users
    b. Ask for honest feedback about what you've missed or misunderstood
    c. Refine based on their experiences, not your assumptions
4. **Identify the most meaningful opportunities**
    a. Which pain points consistently frustrate developers?
    b. Where are the gaps in your critical path that cause developers to drop off (activation)?
    c. How can you reduce the time between starting and experiencing value (time-to-value)?
    d. Which existing touchpoints need improvement or reimagining?
5. **Focus your efforts strategically**
    a. Prioritize fixing issues on the critical path first
    b. Address high-impact problems that can be solved quickly
    c. Develop more comprehensive solutions for complex challenges

Journey mapping becomes powerful when it bridges the gap between how we think developers use our platform and how they actually do it. The insights from this process can transform your DevRel strategy from activity-based to impact-driven.

CREATING YOUR DEVELOPER JOURNEY MAP

Follow these steps to create a comprehensive developer journey map for your platform:

1. Define three to five key developer personas who use your platform. Document their goals, pain points, and primary motivations.
2. List all existing touchpoints developers have with your platform. Organize them into journey phases (Discover, Evaluate, Build, etc.).
3. Identify the key milestones that indicate meaningful progress. Document typical timeframes between points.
4. Create a visual journey map showing all touchpoints and milestones. Use symbols or colors to indicate emotional states. (*Can be pencil and paper for now, whatever is quickest!*)
5. Mark the critical path that represents the minimum viable journey to successful adoption.
6. Analyze your map to identify gaps, points of friction, and opportunities for improvement.
7. Prioritize three to five key opportunities based on their impact on critical path progression.

Lastly, create a simple action plan with specific initiatives to address the top priorities you discovered.

Conclusion: Journey-Driven DevRel

Understanding the developer journey transforms DevRel from a collection of touchpoint activities to a strategic function aligned with developer needs and business outcomes. When you know where developers are coming from, where they're trying to go, and the obstacles they face, you can design interventions that genuinely help them succeed.

Journey mapping provides the essential context for all DevRel initiatives, ensuring they address real developer needs rather than assumed ones. It transforms abstract concepts like "developer experience" into concrete touchpoints and milestones that can be enhanced and measured.

By focusing on the critical path that leads to successful adoption, you ensure your limited resources are invested where they'll have the greatest impact. Rather than trying to improve everything simultaneously, you can strategically focus on removing friction from the most important milestones.

Ultimately, journey-driven DevRel creates a virtuous cycle: as you improve the developer journey, more developers progress successfully, providing more insights that fuel further improvements. This developer-centric approach delivers value to both developers and your business, creating the foundation for sustainable growth and impact.

CHAPTER 4

Filling Gaps in the Developer Journey

In most organizations, no one actually owns the complete developer journey (*an exception here would be developer-first startups at the seed and alpha stages*). Teams focus on their specific areas of ownership, but the spaces between those boundaries often go unnoticed. This chapter focuses on how DevRel can create unique value by identifying and filling these crucial gaps in the developer journey.

Note At AWS, developers told us exactly what they needed. Through conversations and feedback, they made it clear: they wanted more tutorials, sample apps, and practical guides to help them get started. When we mapped ownership across teams, we found that nobody owned this enablement content. Engineering owned reference docs, Marketing owned the blog, but activation content was an open opportunity. Our DevRel team took ownership and created high-quality examples across platforms and languages. After launching this initiative, we saw a 15% month-over-month increase in developer activation. It reinforced that listening to developers and filling the specific gaps they identify is a valuable way for DevRel to create impact.

K. Kemple, *Effective DevRel*, https://doi.org/10.1007/979-8-8688-2373-2_4

Identifying Ownership Gaps Along the Developer Journey

Every organization has these weird spaces where developers get lost—places where nobody has clear ownership or where the team that technically owns something doesn't have the right perspective to make it work for developers. These gaps aren't just problems, though. They're opportunities for your DevRel team to create massive value.

The Ownership Audit

I like to run what I call an "ownership audit" to find these gaps. It's straightforward:

1. Map all touchpoints and milestones from the developer journey.
2. Figure out who currently owns each one.
3. Check metrics and developer feedback for each touchpoint.
4. Flag the problem areas where
    a. Nobody clearly owns it
    b. Someone owns it but doesn't have the resources to do it well
    c. Multiple teams own related pieces but don't coordinate
    d. Developers consistently get lost during handoffs
    e. Developer feedback goes into a black hole

This systematic approach transforms hunches about problem areas into documented evidence you can act on. When you do this kind of audit, patterns start to emerge. You'll spot several types of gaps:

- **Interstitial gaps**: Those spaces between teams where developers fall through the cracks
- **Depth gaps**: Places where basic information exists, but developers need much more

- **Feedback gaps**: Areas where developers give input, but nothing changes
- **Context gaps**: Places where technical information exists without the "why" or "how to apply it"

This becomes your opportunity map. These are the places where you can step in and create value without stepping on toes or duplicating what's already happening.

Strategic Gap Selection

You can't fill every gap you find. You don't have unlimited time, unlimited people, or unlimited budget. You need to be strategic about where you focus. Here's how I think about prioritizing:

1. **Critical path impact:** Does this gap affect a major milestone on the path to adoption?
2. **Developer pain level:** How much are developers actually struggling because of this gap?
3. **Business alignment:** Will fixing this gap move the needle on what your company cares about?
4. **Resource reality:** Can your team realistically take this on without burning out?
5. **Organizational relationships:** Can you address this gap in a way that builds bridges rather than walls?

The sweet spot is finding those high-impact gaps that cause real developer pain, align with business goals, fit within your resources, and let you collaborate positively with other teams. Those are the gaps where you can create massive value that everyone recognizes.

Mapping Organizational Ownership

Time to get practical about mapping ownership across the organization. The goal isn't to create territorial battles but to understand who's already responsible for what, so you can find the spaces where you can add unique value.

Identifying Hidden Assumptions

Before you can map ownership effectively, you need to uncover the hidden assumptions that create gaps in the first place. Many ownership gaps result from assumptions across the organization:

- Product assumes Marketing is educating developers about feature benefits.
- Marketing assumes Engineering is creating technical tutorials.
- Engineering assumes Product is defining developer personas and journeys.
- Everyone assumes someone else is connecting the dots.

These assumptions create invisible gaps that directly impact the developer experience. By surfacing these assumptions through cross-functional conversations, you can identify opportunities where DevRel can add unique value.

The most dangerous assumption? That developers will figure it out on their own. They might, eventually. But every moment they spend confused or searching for answers is a moment they're not building with your platform. That's lost value for them and your business.

Milestone Transition Analysis

Once you understand the assumptions at play, examine how they affect the developer journey. Focus on how developers move between critical milestones:

1. **From awareness to first exploration**: Who helps developers move from discovering your platform to taking their first concrete steps?
2. **From exploration to creating their first application**: Who guides developers from initial tinkering to building something meaningful?

3. **From first application to deeper integration**: Who supports developers as they expand beyond basic examples to real implementation?
4. **From development to production deployment**: Who helps developers bridge the often-challenging gap between working code and production systems?
5. **From basic usage to advanced capabilities**: Who shows developers how to level up from basic features to more sophisticated use cases?
6. **From individual usage to team adoption**: Who facilitates the spread of your technology within organizations?

This milestone-focused approach often reveals that even when touchpoints have clear owners, the transitions between milestones remain unowned. Developers frequently get lost in these "between spaces" where they need to connect knowledge from multiple sources to make progress. DevRel can create tremendous value by focusing on these transition points, helping developers successfully move from one milestone to the next through integrated guidance.

Touchpoint Ownership Matrix

Now that you understand the assumptions and transition gaps, document your findings in a practical tool. Create a simple matrix that maps each developer touchpoint against its current ownership status and contribution opportunities:

Touchpoint	Ownership Status	How DevRel Can Contribute	Gap Type
Documentation	Owned by Engineering	Add real-world examples, provide developer feedback	Depth gap
API Reference	Owned by Engineering	Create tutorials that complement reference material	Connection gap
Blog	Owned by Marketing	Contribute technical deep dives, developer success stories	Context gap
Community Forums	Owned by Support	Identify patterns, create content addressing common questions	Feedback gap
Sample Applications	Not clearly owned	Create and maintain consistent examples across platforms	Ownership gap
Developer Onboarding	Partially owned by multiple teams	Create a cohesive journey connecting different pieces	Connection gap

This visualization helps you spot complete ownership gaps where no team clearly owns a critical touchpoint, connection gaps where touchpoints exist but lack cohesion, depth gaps where touchpoints could benefit from DevRel expertise, and contribution opportunities where DevRel can enhance existing touchpoints.

When mapping ownership, think beyond formal responsibility. Sometimes, a team might technically own something on paper but lacks the resources or bandwidth to give it proper attention. Those situations create natural opportunities for supportive collaboration. The matrix becomes your strategic planning tool, turning theoretical understanding into actionable opportunities.

Contributing to Owned Touchpoints

I want to be super clear about something. DevRel isn't just about finding unowned spaces. Some of your most valuable work happens when you contribute to touchpoints that already have owners. This approach is all about partnership, not competition.

Becoming a Value-Adding Partner

When you find touchpoints with established owners, think about how you can make their work even better:

1. **Start with genuine appreciation.** Seriously, recognize the good stuff they're already doing. This isn't just politics. It's about building real relationships.

2. **Offer specific value.** Don't just say "We could help," but rather "We could contribute these specific things."

3. **Focus on shared goals.** Frame everything in terms of what you both care about.

4. **Show respect for their ownership.** Make it clear you're there to support, not take over.

Let me give you a real example. Say documentation is owned by Engineering. Instead of criticizing the gap or trying to take over documentation, you might

- Offer to collect and share real developer feedback on the docs
- Create tutorial content that complements their reference material
- Build real-world examples showing how to apply their documentation
- Connect them directly with developers for insights

See the difference? You're making their documentation more valuable while building a positive relationship. They start seeing you as an ally who makes them look good, not a threat who wants their job.

Small Wins for Building Trust

Here's my secret for building amazing cross-team relationships: start small and make people look good. Trust doesn't happen overnight. It builds through a series of small, successful collaborations that benefit everyone involved:

1. Find quick, easy opportunities where you can add obvious value with minimal coordination.

2. Execute improvements that don't need fifteen approvals and six months of planning.
3. Measure what happened and share those results.
4. Make sure everyone involved gets credit for the success.

Let me show you what this looks like. Say you notice the Marketing blog doesn't have much developer-focused content. You could

- Offer to write a technical post that supports their upcoming campaign
- Volunteer to review their existing content for technical accuracy
- Share specific feedback from developers about what content they'd find valuable
- Track and share how the technical content performs compared to other posts

These small wins show you can deliver value. They start to trust your judgment, which opens doors for bigger collaborations. Before you know it, you've gone from outsider to trusted partner without any territorial battles.

Progressive Partnership Model

As trust builds, you can evolve partnerships through progressive stages:

1. **Advisory relationship**: Providing input and feedback on existing touchpoints
2. **Contributory relationship**: Actively adding content or capabilities to touchpoints
3. **Collaborative relationship**: Jointly planning and executing touchpoint improvements
4. **Strategic alliance**: Developing shared ownership models for critical touchpoints

Each stage deepens the partnership while creating more value for developers and the business. The key is patience. You can't jump straight to a strategic alliance. You earn your way there through consistent value delivery and relationship building.

Creating Your Strategic Position

With a clear understanding of ownership gaps and partnership opportunities, you can now define DevRel's unique position within your organization.

The DevRel Positioning Statement

Create a clear statement that captures

1. **Primary focus areas**: The parts of the developer journey that you own or heavily influence
2. **Key outcomes**: The specific metrics and results you commit to delivering
3. **Organizational relationships**: How you complement and support other functions
4. **Resource boundaries**: What you explicitly don't own or prioritize

This statement clarifies roles for your team and stakeholders, preventing scope creep and misaligned expectations. It becomes your north star when every urgent request tries to pull you in different directions.

Building Your Positioning Narrative

Effective positioning requires more than a statement. You need a compelling narrative that explains

1. **Why these gaps matter**: The impact on developers and business outcomes
2. **Why DevRel is uniquely suited**: The specific capabilities that make DevRel the right function to address these gaps
3. **How success will be measured**: Clear metrics and milestones that demonstrate impact
4. **What resources are required**: Realistic assessment of what's needed to succeed

This narrative helps stakeholders understand the strategic value of your positioning and builds support for your approach. Without it, you're just another team asking for budget and headcount.

Communicating Your Position

Once defined, your positioning needs effective communication:

1. **Leadership alignment:** Ensure executive sponsors understand and support your focus.
2. **Cross-functional clarity**: Communicate your role to adjacent teams.
3. **Team understanding**: Make sure your own team understands the strategic focus.
4. **Regular reinforcement**: Continue to refer to your positioning when discussing priorities and resources.

Clear, consistent communication prevents misunderstandings and helps maintain focus on your strategic gaps. Every time someone asks, "Why is DevRel doing this?", you should have a clear answer that ties back to your positioning.

The Iterative Position

DevRel's position isn't static. It should evolve as the organization and market mature. Review and refine your positioning

- **Quarterly**: Adjust focus areas based on business priorities and developer needs.
- **Annually**: Reassess fundamental assumptions about ownership and scope.
- **At major inflection points**: Re-evaluate after significant company changes, product pivots, or market shifts.

This flexibility allows DevRel to remain relevant and impactful as the context changes. What matters in a startup won't be the same as what matters in a scale-up or enterprise.

Initiating Cross-Functional Conversations

The way you approach cross-functional conversations significantly impacts your ability to fill ownership gaps effectively. This isn't about demanding territory. It's about building collaborative relationships that enhance the developer experience.

Starting with Shared Goals

Begin conversations by establishing common ground:

1. **Connect to developer success**: Frame discussions around improving the developer experience.
2. **Link to business outcomes**: Identify how improved experiences drive business metrics.
3. **Acknowledge existing efforts**: Recognize the good work already happening.
4. **Focus on complementary capabilities**: Emphasize how different functions bring unique strengths.

This approach shifts conversations from potential turf battles to collaborative problem-solving. Nobody wants to fight over territory. Everyone wants developers to succeed.

The Value-First Approach

When approaching other teams, lead with the value you can provide:

1. **Bring developer insights**: Share specific feedback from developers that helps inform their work.
2. **Offer specialized skills**: Identify capabilities your team has that complement their strengths.
3. **Reduce their workload**: Find ways to take on tasks that burden them but align with your expertise.
4. **Amplify their impact**: Show how DevRel can extend the reach and effectiveness of their efforts.

When people experience tangible benefits from working with DevRel, they become champions for collaboration rather than defenders of territory.

Building Relationships Before Needs

The worst time to establish a relationship is when you urgently need something. Instead

1. **Invest in ongoing connections:** Build relationships during peacetime, not just when issues arise.
2. **Understand their challenges:** Learn what pressures and metrics drive other teams.
3. **Celebrate their successes:** Be a genuine champion for their accomplishments.
4. **Find informal touchpoints:** Connect outside formal meetings to build authentic relationships.

These relationship investments create the foundation for effective collaboration when addressing ownership gaps. The best time to build a bridge is before you need to cross the river.

The Language of Contribution

The language you use significantly impacts how your intentions are perceived.

Table 4-2.

Instead of saying...	Try saying...
We should own this	How can we contribute to this?
This isn't working	What outcomes are we trying to achieve?
We need to take this over	Where can we support you?
You should change this	Developers have been sharing feedback about...

Language that focuses on contribution rather than criticism builds receptivity to your ideas. People want to work with partners, not critics.

DEFINING YOUR STRATEGIC POSITION

Grab a coffee and set aside 30 minutes to work through this exercise. It will transform vague ideas about DevRel positioning into a concrete strategy for your specific situation:

1. List three to five developer journey touchpoints that nobody clearly owns in your organization right now.
2. Rate each touchpoint from 1–5 on its impact on developer success, business outcomes, and strategic priorities.
3. Identify two to three touchpoints that already have owners where your DevRel team could add significant value as a partner.
4. Write a positioning statement that clearly defines which ownership gaps your DevRel team will fill, how you'll partner on existing touchpoints, what specific metrics this positioning will improve, and what resources you'll need to make this happen.

Lastly, outline how you'll communicate this position to executive leadership, partner teams, and your DevRel team.

Conclusion: From Uncertainty to Strategic Clarity

Finding your unique position in an organization can feel like navigating without a map. You want to create value without stepping on toes, contribute without competing, and fill gaps without creating tension. It's a delicate balance that keeps many DevRel teams stuck in reactive mode.

When you identify those ownership gaps nobody else is filling, you transform DevRel from something vague and hard to define into a strategic function everyone values. You stop wondering where you fit and start creating connections nobody else is making.

This clarity makes everything better. Your team understands what to focus on and why it matters. Your organization sees DevRel's unique value. Most importantly, developers get a more coherent experience that actually helps them succeed.

The most effective DevRel teams don't try to own everything. They identify where they can create unique value and build partnerships that enhance the entire developer journey. They find the gaps everyone else misses and fill them with expertise and genuine empathy for developers.

When you apply these approaches, you position DevRel as an essential bridge between different parts of the organization. You become the connective tissue that helps everyone work better together rather than just another team competing for attention and resources.

With this foundation of strategic positioning, you're ready to build on the operational excellence, measurement approaches, and leadership strategies that will bring your Developer Relations work to life. The clarity you've gained about your unique position becomes the platform for everything else you'll accomplish.

PART II

Maximizing Developer Enablement

CHAPTER 5

Making Developer Engagements Meaningful

Creating content is one of the fundamental responsibilities of Developer Relations. It extends your reach beyond in-person connections, scales your expertise to thousands of developers simultaneously, and serves developers throughout their journey with your platform. While documentation provides the essential foundation, effective DevRel requires a diverse content portfolio that addresses different learning styles, use cases, and developer journey stages.

The most impactful developer content directly addresses developer needs while supporting business goals. This balanced approach requires understanding developers' challenges and contexts alongside your company's strategic priorities. When content successfully bridges these perspectives, it creates a win-win scenario—developers get genuinely helpful resources that solve their problems, and your business drives meaningful platform adoption.

Effective developer content requires intentional choices around topics, formats, and distribution channels. Success comes from maximizing the return on your content investments.

Note If you look at the book's outline, you'll see that AI is discussed only in a specific section. That was an intentional choice! AI is still rapidly evolving, so mixing that topic throughout the other chapters, instead of organizing it all together, would make this book time-bound and require significant effort to constantly update. By isolating it to a section of one chapter, I can inform readers that the section may become quickly outdated and make targeted updates to just that section when there are enough new advancements to share.

K. Kemple, *Effective DevRel*, https://doi.org/10.1007/979-8-8688-2373-2_5

Identifying High-Impact Content Opportunities

Finding the right content to create feels a bit like being a detective. You're constantly gathering clues from everywhere—inside companies and out in the wild with developers. It's this beautiful dance between what developers are desperately searching for and what your company needs them to discover.

Different signals help identify content needs. Support teams field recurring questions, user feedback highlights pain points, and analytics show where users get stuck. Meanwhile, product teams release new features, and marketing develops fresh messaging that needs to be incorporated.

The real impact happens when internal and external worlds overlap—those times when what developers need to know and what your company needs them to know are actually the same thing. That's the content goldmine we're all searching for.

Finding the Signal in the Noise

The most impactful content balances genuine developer needs with organizational priorities. Neither should be ignored. The sweet spot lies in identifying where they align. To find this balance

1. **Analyze support channels:** What questions appear repeatedly in forums and support tickets?

2. **Monitor social conversations:** What challenges do developers mention when discussing your technology?

3. **Review documentation feedback:** Which pages see the most traffic? Where do developers spend the most time?

4. **Review search analytics:** What terms do developers search for most frequently?

5. **Analyze developer journey gaps:** Where do developers get stuck or drop off in their learning path?

6. **Check with partners:** What content requests have come in from cross-functional partners?

7. **Understand business objectives:** Which features, use cases, or adoption paths are strategic priorities?

8. **Identify alignment points:** Where do developer needs and organizational goals naturally intersect?

As you collect these signals, maintain a dedicated "content ideas" repository where you can track and prioritize potential topics. This prevents great ideas from slipping through the cracks and gives you a pool of options to draw from when planning your content calendar. The best DevRel teams build systems for capturing these insights rather than relying on memory or scattered notes.

Content That Moves the Needle

Not all content is created equal. Some content types directly impact developer progression through the journey, while others primarily serve awareness or support functions. When prioritizing your content investments, consider these high-impact opportunities.

Activation Content

Content that helps developers achieve their first meaningful success with your platform often delivers the highest return on investment. This includes

- Quick-start guides that lead to working implementations
- Sample applications that developers can modify for their needs
- Interactive tutorials that provide guided experiences

After all, no matter the persona, every developer needs to onboard to your platform.

Friction-Reducing Content

Content that addresses known friction points can significantly help developers reach the next milestone on their journey:

- Troubleshooting guides for common error scenarios
- Migration guides for moving between versions or from competitors
- Integration patterns for connecting with popular technologies

When prioritizing where you should focus, look for high-friction, high-opportunity points along the developer journey.

Feature Adoption Content

Content that promotes the adoption of strategic features can align perfectly with business objectives:

- Use-case examples showing the value of premium features
- Solution patterns that incorporate new capabilities
- Performance comparisons demonstrating advantages over alternatives

By focusing your limited resources on these high-impact areas, you create content that serves both developers and your business effectively.

Choosing Cost-Effective Content Formats

Developers learn differently, and various concepts lend themselves to specific presentation formats. Equally important is being smart about where you invest your limited content creation time. The right format isn't just about what works best for developers—it's also about what you can realistically produce with the resources you have.

The Minimum Viable Format

When faced with tight deadlines or urgent content needs, focus on the lowest time-cost format that will still effectively achieve your content objectives:

- Instead of a full-length tutorial, consider a focused blog post highlighting key steps.
- Rather than a polished video, create a simple screen recording with a voice-over.
- In place of a comprehensive guide, publish a targeted FAQ addressing the most critical questions.

This approach ensures you can respond to urgent content needs without sacrificing quality or missing critical relevance windows. You can always replace them with more polished, time-intensive content in the future.

Choosing the Right Formats for the Right Job

To maximize developer engagement and learning, it's important to tailor your content format to both your objectives and available resources. Different formats serve different purposes in your content ecosystem:

- Written content
    - **Blog posts:** Best for announcements, perspectives, and success stories
    - **Tutorials:** Best for step-by-step learning experiences
    - **Newsletters:** Best for regular updates, curated resources, and community highlights
- Visual content
    - **Diagrams:** Best for architecture, workflows, and system relationships
    - **Screenshots and GIFs:** Best for UI interactions, configuration steps, and visual confirmation
- Video content
    - **Tutorials:** Best for complex processes with visual components
    - **Webinars:** Best for comprehensive topic exploration and community engagement
- Audio content
    - **Podcasts:** Perfect for discussions, interviews, and deeper dives
    - **LinkedIn Lives:** Great for casual Q&A sessions and relationship building
- Interactive content
    - **Live streams:** Best for real-time problem-solving and unscripted learning
    - **Workshops:** Best for comprehensive skill-building in a structured environment

Pick formats that match your goals and what you have to work with while meeting developers where they are. This lets you make the best use of your time and resources.

The Format Decision Framework

Before creating content, ask yourself these key questions to determine the most appropriate format:

- **What's the shelf life of this information?**
    - Content that needs frequent updates may not be ideal for video.
    - Blog posts and documentation offer more flexibility for updates.
- **How specialized is this knowledge?**
    - Niche topics may not justify the high production costs of video.
    - Very specific technical details might be better served by focused written content.
- **What's your timeline?**
    - Tight deadlines typically rule out using more time-intensive formats.
    - When pressed for time, identify the "minimum viable format."

The most effective content strategies blend these formats strategically, matching each topic to its most appropriate delivery mechanism while considering resource constraints.

Balancing Technical Expertise with Accessibility

Writing technical content presents two key challenges. You need to maintain a deep technical understanding of complex topics while also developing strong communication skills to translate that expertise to your audience effectively. Success requires mastering both of these essential abilities.

From Technical Understanding to Effective Communication

Technical knowledge alone isn't enough for great content. The hallmark of effective technical writing is translating complex concepts into accessible explanations. To bridge this gap

- **Know your audience:** Adapt explanations based on technical background and learning preferences.
- **Develop a metaphor library:** Collect analogies and mental models that clarify complex concepts.
- **Practice progressive disclosure:** Layer information from the most straightforward application to a deeper understanding.
- **Incorporate visual thinking:** Use diagrams and visual representations to clarify relationships.
- **Test explanations:** Validate your explanations with developers from your target audience.

Perhaps the most valuable skill in content creation is the ability to translate complex technical concepts into accessible explanations while maintaining accuracy.

Finding Your Unique Position on the Spectrum

Rather than trying to excel equally at everything, recognize your natural strengths and build around them:

- Are you strongest in technical depth, communication clarity, or structural organization?
- Do you excel at procedural documentation, conceptual explanations, or reference material?
- Are you most effective with beginners, intermediate users, or advanced practitioners?

By understanding your specific strengths, you can focus on contexts where you add unique value while collaborating with others whose strengths complement yours. This self-awareness leads to more effective technical writing teams with balanced capabilities.

A quick note on becoming indispensable: While developing deep expertise is important, be careful not to become the only person who can create effective content. As the chapter on team structure explains, being a "keystone" team member creates risk for both you and your organization. Make sure you're documenting your approaches and helping others develop similar skills.

The Technical Currency Challenge

Technology evolves rapidly, and staying current requires intentional effort. To maintain your technical edge for effective writing

1. **Schedule hands-on time:** Block regular calendar time for coding, experimenting, and building.
2. **Create learning projects:** Develop personal projects that stretch your skills in relevant directions.
3. **Learning in public:** Create content or examples showcasing your learning experience.
4. **Join internal technical discussions:** Participate in engineering meetings and design reviews.
5. **Follow primary sources:** Read release notes, RFCs, and technical specifications directly.
6. **Build alongside documentation:** As you create guides, actually build what you're documenting.

Without this deliberate practice, your technical knowledge gradually becomes theoretical rather than practical, undermining your credibility and effectiveness in your content.

Creating Use Case-Driven Examples for Developers

Generic content rarely drives action. Developers engage most deeply with content that addresses specific, practical use cases they recognize from their work.

For example, instead of documenting messaging capabilities in isolation, create content showing how those capabilities enable

- Implementing a notification system for a mobile application
- Building a real-time collaboration feature
- Creating an event-driven microservices architecture

This use-case approach connects abstract capabilities to concrete value, making it easier for developers to see how your technology solves their problems.

The Anatomy of Effective Examples

The most compelling examples share key characteristics:

1. Examples should be simple enough to understand but realistic enough to be credible.
2. Include all necessary setup, dependencies, and configuration.
3. Frame examples within a use-case narrative:
    a. What problem does this example solve?
    b. Why would a developer choose this approach?
    c. What limitations should be noted?
4. Start with fundamental patterns before introducing more sophisticated approaches.

From Code Snippets to Sample Applications

Providing developers with relevant, scenario-driven examples is essential for effective technical documentation. Generic content rarely drives action. Developers engage most deeply with content that addresses specific, practical use cases they recognize from their work. Different scenarios call for different types of examples:

- Code Snippets
    - **Best for:** Illustrating specific, more granular examples.
    - **Context:** Provide enough surrounding code for a clear understanding. Include imports, error handling, and expected behavior.
- Sample Applications
    - **Best for:** Illustrating big-picture, more complete examples.
    - **Structure:** Well-organized, well-documented codebases following best practices. Include dependencies, tests, CI/CD, and expected behavior.

By focusing on realistic, well-structured examples, you help bridge abstract concepts with practical solutions. As you move forward, consider how to design adaptable examples that empower developers to tailor solutions to their unique needs.

Making Examples Adaptable

The most valuable examples serve as starting points for developers' work. Design examples with adaptation in mind:

1. **Modular structure:** Organize code so developers can easily extract and repurpose components.
2. **Clear separation of concerns:** Distinguish between core functionality and example-specific elements.
3. **Configuration externalization:** Allow key variables to be easily modified through configuration.

When developers can readily adapt your examples to their specific needs, adoption accelerates, and your content creates greater value.

Building Quality Workshops

Workshops represent one of the most effective (and most challenging) forms of developer content. They combine technical education with real-time interaction, providing guided experiences that accelerate adoption.

Designing Effective Workshop Experiences

The best workshops follow principles similar to the Understanding by Design framework—starting with clear outcomes in mind and working backward. Instead of just throwing a bunch of technical information at people, think about what you want them to be able to do when they walk out the door.

1. **Begin with the end in mind:** What specific capabilities should participants have after your workshop? What should they understand deeply enough to apply later?
2. **Determine evidence of understanding:** How will you know if participants really "got it"? What will they create or demonstrate?

3. **Plan learning experiences accordingly:** Only after defining outcomes and evidence should you design the specific activities and content.

This backward design approach ensures your workshop stays focused on meaningful learning rather than just covering material.

Balancing Structure and Exploration

Effective workshops balance structured guidance with opportunities for discovery:

- Guided sections provide step-by-step instructions:
    - Clear, numbered steps with expected outcomes
    - Explanations of why each step matters
    - Troubleshooting guidance for common issues
- Explorative sections encourage applying knowledge to novel situations:
    - Open-ended challenges with defined objectives but multiple solution paths
    - Prompts to modify and extend examples

This balance prevents workshops from becoming rigid follow-along sessions or overwhelming free-for-alls. Like in good instructional design, you scaffold the learning, providing structure where needed but gradually removing it as developers build confidence.

Technical Environment Considerations

High-quality developer content goes far beyond simple documentation—it's about creating engaging, hands-on experiences that foster real understanding and adoption. Workshops are a prime example, blending technical instruction with interactive learning to empower developers and drive meaningful results. In this section, we'll explore how to design and deliver impactful workshops that truly resonate with your audience. Workshop environments present unique technical challenges:

1. **Minimize setup friction:** Pre-configured cloud environments, containerized development environments, and sandbox environments for your product.

2. **Build resilience:** Provide backup access methods, create completed milestones that skip problematic sections (like infrastructure or authentication setup, unless critical to the workshop goals), and have troubleshooting guides ready.

3. **Plan for the unexpected:** Always have a backup plan when live demos go wrong (and they will!).

By thoughtfully designing workshops with clear goals, structured guidance, and flexible exploration, you create an environment where meaningful learning can flourish. Addressing technical challenges up front further ensures participants can focus on gaining practical experience, rather than troubleshooting setup issues. Ultimately, a well-crafted workshop not only imparts knowledge but also empowers developers to confidently apply what they've learned in real-world scenarios.

Content Distribution and Repurposing

Content creation doesn't end with initial development. An effective content strategy includes thoughtful adaptation across different formats and channels, maximizing reach and impact.

Content Transformation Strategies

Successfully reaching your audience requires more than just creating great content—it demands smart strategies for sharing and adapting that material. One practice you should standardize is transforming existing material to reach different audiences:

- **Blog posts to videos:** Use the blog post's structure as the video script and add visual demonstrations.
- **Webinars to blog posts:** Capture key points and expand on questions that arose during the session.
- **Documentation for workshops:** Extract key concepts and develop hands-on exercises.
- **Long-form content to social media:** Extract key insights or interesting code snippets with visual elements.

By intentionally planning and adapting your content approach, you set the foundation for meaningful engagement, sustained platform growth, and a developer community that feels supported and inspired. Remember, the effort invested in thoughtful content planning pays dividends in adoption, advocacy, and long-term success.

Choosing Effective Distribution Channels

The most effective channel strategy matches each content type to the most suitable channels, taking into account not just the format but also where your target developers actually spend their time. This means carefully assessing the unique strengths of each platform—such as technical forums, social networks, or partner newsletters—and aligning your distribution plan with developers' real-world habits and preferences.

By meeting your audience where they are most active and engaged, you ensure your content is seen, valued, and acted upon, ultimately maximizing its impact. Some common conversion paths are

1. **Platform-owned channels:** Documentation portals, developer portals, blogs, newsletters
2. **Developer community channels:** Stack Overflow, GitHub, Reddit, Discord
3. **Social platforms:** Bluesky, LinkedIn, Dev.to
4. **Events and conferences:** Virtual and in-person opportunities
5. **Partner channels:** Cross-promotional opportunities with ecosystem partners

Creating valuable content is only half the battle. Getting it in front of the right developers is equally important.

Implementing a Content Pipeline

Establish a centralized space where all drafts, finalized pieces, and supporting resources are stored before they're released. This allows you to streamline collaboration, organize your workflow, and ensure every item is reviewed and ready for distribution—making the publishing process smoother and more strategic. Separate writing from publishing by building a content repository:

1. **Create dedicated content sprints:** Schedule focused periods where team members concentrate primarily on content creation.
2. **Implement staged review processes:** Separate content creation, technical review, and final approval into distinct stages.
3. **Maintain content freshness:** Regularly review content in your repository to ensure it remains technically accurate, updating or deprecating content as needed.

This approach transforms content creation from a reactive, pressure-filled activity into a strategic, manageable process.

DEVELOP YOUR CONTENT PLAN

This structured exercise will help you put your content strategy knowledge into practice. Work through each step to create a comprehensive content plan for your developer platform.

1. Review your current content and make a list of what you have (documentation, blog posts, videos, etc.).
2. List three current business objectives (features, use cases, adoption paths, etc.).
3. List any known content needs (use the developer journey to understand where there may be gaps).
4. List five essential pieces of content you need to create based on your lists.
5. Choose the format you think will best serve each content piece (if you're transforming content, think through how you might approach it).
6. Choose your main distribution channel for each content piece.
7. Create a simple timeline for the next three months of content.
8. Identify who will create each piece of content.

Review this plan quarterly to ensure your content strategy stays aligned with developer needs and business goals.

Conclusion: Content As a Strategic Investment

Effective content creation isn't an afterthought—it's a strategic investment that drives platform adoption, reduces support costs, and builds developer relationships. When approached systematically, content becomes one of the highest-leverage activities in Developer Relations.

The most successful DevRel teams treat content as a product with intentional design and continuous improvement. By selecting topics that balance developer needs with business goals, choosing appropriate formats, creating practical examples, and incorporating feedback, you transform content from a cost center into a strategic asset that accelerates developer success and platform growth.

Remember that content is often the first and most frequent way developers interact with your platform. Every piece of content shapes their perception and influences their journey. By applying the principles in this chapter, you create content that doesn't just inform—it enables, inspires, and drives meaningful adoption.

CHAPTER 6

Creating Effective Content

Documentation isn't a project with a finish line—it's an ongoing commitment that expands and evolves alongside your product. Without a systematic approach, you'll constantly feel underwater, struggling to balance quality with speed and thoroughness with clarity.

But here's the good news: you don't need to reinvent the wheel every time. With the right frameworks and systems, you can create documentation that serves developers with different learning styles, addresses various journey stages, and can be maintained without heroic effort. That's what this chapter explores—transforming documentation from an overwhelming burden into a sustainable practice that dramatically increases your impact.

Meeting Core Developer Needs

Not all documentation serves the same purpose. Treating all technical content as interchangeable leads to confusion and frustration for both creators and users. The most effective technical documentation recognizes distinct types, each serving a different developer need.

This approach aligns with the Diátaxis framework, which organizes documentation by user needs rather than product features. (You'll find more details about this framework in the Resources appendix.)

Let's explore these four documentation types and how they serve distinct developer needs throughout their journey.

K. Kemple, *Effective DevRel*, https://doi.org/10.1007/979-8-8688-2373-2_6

Tutorials: Learning-Oriented Content

Tutorials guide newcomers through their first interactions with your technology. They're deliberately structured learning experiences with these key characteristics:

1. They focus on helping the developer accomplish a concrete, meaningful task.
2. They follow a clear sequence without branching paths.
3. They introduce concepts only when needed to complete the task.
4. They ensure the developer experiences a "win" by the conclusion.

Effective tutorials anticipate common stumbling blocks and provide enough guidance to keep developers moving forward without overwhelming them with details. They build confidence and create positive first impressions of your technology.

Think of tutorials as guided journeys with a supportive instructor. The developer isn't yet comfortable exploring on their own—they need a carefully constructed path that leads to success while building their understanding. Tutorials create that crucial foundation of confidence that transforms uncertain beginners into explorers ready to dive deeper.

How-To Guides: Problem-Oriented Content

How-to guides address specific tasks that developers need to accomplish. Unlike tutorials, they assume some baseline knowledge and focus entirely on solving a particular problem:

1. Each guide tackles one discrete task.
2. The structure focuses on achieving a specific outcome.
3. Instructions are straightforward with minimal theoretical background.
4. Guides can acknowledge alternative approaches when relevant.

How-to guides are reliable references for developers who know what they want to do but need guidance on how to do it. They're direct, practical, and focused on immediate developer needs.

While tutorials are about learning, how-to guides are about achieving. They serve developers who have a specific goal in mind and need the steps to achieve it. Think of how-to guides as recipes in a cookbook—the developer already understands the basics of cooking; they're looking for specific instructions for a particular dish.

Reference: Information-Oriented Content

Reference documentation provides comprehensive technical details about your platform's components, APIs, classes, functions, and configuration options. Effective reference material

1. Includes all available options and parameters
2. Maintains consistent structure for similar elements
3. Focuses on precise, concise, and neutral descriptions
4. Organizes information for rapid lookup, not sequential reading

Reference material serves as the single source of truth for technical details. Developers rely on it when they know what they're using but need specific information about usage, parameters, or return values.

Reference documentation is all about precision and completeness. It's not meant to be read from start to finish but rather consulted when specific questions arise. If tutorials are like classroom lessons and how-to guides are like recipes, reference documentation is like a dictionary or encyclopedia—it's authoritative, thorough, and organized for quick access rather than narrative flow.

Explanation: Understanding-Oriented Content

Explanation content illuminates the "why" behind the "how." It provides conceptual insight and theoretical background:

1. It helps developers build mental models of how things work.
2. It explains design decisions, architectural approaches, and underlying principles.
3. It shows how different components relate to each other.
4. It helps developers make better decisions through conceptual clarity.

Explanation content isn't about immediate task completion—it focuses on building deeper knowledge that enables developers to make better architectural and implementation choices.

Explanations address the deeper questions that naturally arise as developers gain experience with your platform. They go beyond immediate functionality to help developers understand the underlying systems. This understanding transforms developers from script-followers into creative problem-solvers who can apply your platform to novel challenges. If tutorials are about "how to do," explanations are about "how to think" about your technology.

Building Practical Learning Paths

Developers learn differently and come to your platform with varying levels of experience. Creating effective learning paths accommodates these differences while guiding developers toward proficiency with your technology.

Supporting Nonlinear Learning Journeys

The developer journey is rarely linear. As we explored in Chapter 3, developers rarely follow a predictable path from beginner to expert. Their learning process jumps between different needs and modes depending on their immediate goals, prior experience, and working context.

Your documentation structure needs to support this nonlinear reality. Rather than forcing developers through a predetermined sequence, effective documentation recognizes that different documentation types serve different needs that can arise at any point in the developer's journey:

- A senior engineer might need a tutorial when first encountering your platform.
- A newcomer might dive straight into reference documentation to solve a specific problem.
- The same developer might need explanatory content in the morning and how-to guides in the afternoon.

The beauty of well-structured documentation is that it meets developers wherever they are at any moment. Effective documentation accommodates all these approaches while making it easy to move between different content types as needs change.

When creating these learning paths, think about the questions developers are likely to ask at each stage:

- **Beginners ask:** "How do I get started?"
- **Implementers ask:** "How do I accomplish this specific task?"
- **Troubleshooters ask:** "What does this error mean?"
- **Extenders ask:** "How can I adapt this for my unique case?"
- **Experts ask:** "Why was it designed this way?"

By anticipating these questions and creating clear paths between different documentation types, you create an experience that feels responsive to developer needs at every stage of their journey.

Connecting Documentation Types

While each documentation type has a distinct purpose, effective technical writing creates clear connections between them:

1. Tutorials should link to relevant how-to and conceptual guides for developers who want to customize or extend what they've learned.
2. How-to guides should reference the API documentation for deeper details.
3. Reference material should provide links to conceptual explanations.
4. Explanations should connect to practical how-to guides that demonstrate concepts in action.

These connections create a web of knowledge that developers can navigate according to their current needs rather than forcing them into rigid learning paths.

Think of these connections as helpful signposts that guide developers to what they need next. When a developer completes a tutorial, they're likely wondering, "What else can I do with this?" That's the perfect moment to point them toward related how-to guides. When they're reading reference documentation and wonder why something works a certain way, a link to an explanation provides that deeper context.

Accommodating Different Skill Levels

Developers approach your platform with widely varying expertise. Your documentation should serve everyone from beginners to experts:

1. Create explicit beginner paths that assume minimal prior knowledge.
2. Develop intermediate content that builds on foundational concepts.
3. Provide advanced documentation for experienced users seeking optimization.
4. Label content clearly with the prerequisite knowledge, tools, or accounts they may need.

This tiered approach ensures that newcomers aren't overwhelmed while experienced developers can quickly find the depth they need. Remember that even expert developers are beginners when they first encounter your platform.

The ability to skim is crucial for experienced developers. They need to quickly assess what they already know and focus on what's new or different about your platform. Using consistent structures, clear headings, and progressive disclosure allows them to navigate efficiently. At the same time, beginners need comprehensive guidance that doesn't assume prior knowledge. By being explicit about prerequisites and providing clear learning paths, you help developers at all levels find their optimal entry point.

Techniques for Effective Technical Writing

Writing clear, accurate documentation is both an art and a science. These practical techniques will help you create content that resonates with developers and genuinely helps them succeed.

Writing for Developer Audiences

Developers have distinct needs and expectations when consuming technical content. Here's how effective technical writing addresses these needs through intentional choices:

- Core principles for developer documentation:
    - Write with straightforward language and direct sentences.
    - Maintain consistent terminology throughout.
    - Organize information in predictable, meaningful patterns.
    - Provide code examples alongside explanations.
    - Consider that many readers use English as a second language.
- Key goals when writing for developers:
    - Reduce cognitive load.
    - Frontload essential information.
    - Use consistent patterns.
    - Avoid unnecessary prose.
    - Provide immediate answers with optional context.

Remember that technical accuracy alone isn't enough. Documentation can be perfectly correct yet practically useless if it fails to connect with developers' actual needs and contexts. The most effective technical writing combines precision with empathy—understanding not just what your technology does, but how developers will actually use it in their daily work. It also helps to maintain a style guide for your documentation, ensuring consistency across authors.

From Technical Understanding to Effective Communication

Technical knowledge alone isn't enough for great content. You need to translate complex concepts into accessible explanations:

1. Know your personas and adapt explanations based on their specific contexts.
2. Develop metaphors and mental models that clarify complex concepts.
3. Layer information from basic application to deeper understanding.
4. Use diagrams and visual representations to clarify relationships.
5. Test your explanations with developers from your target audience.

The most valuable skill in technical writing is translating complexity into clarity without sacrificing accuracy. This balance allows developers to learn and apply your technology efficiently.

People often assume technical writing is primarily about technical knowledge, but communication skills are equally important. The best technical writers aren't necessarily the deepest technical experts—they're the people who can bridge the gap between expert knowledge and developer understanding.

Hands-On Validation: Writing from Experience

Validating your documentation through hands-on testing is the single most important quality practice you can implement. The "blank environment" test is your most powerful tool for ensuring documentation quality.

Here's how to perform a blank environment test:

- Set up a fresh environment matching what a developer would use.
- Follow your own instructions exactly as written.
- Document any confusion or missing steps.
- Revise your content accordingly.
- Repeat until everything works flawlessly.

This process is crucial because technical experts often accumulate tacit knowledge that shapes their understanding. You might automatically

- Set specific environment variables
- Use particular software versions
- Follow certain practices without thinking
- Skip steps that seem "obvious"

A developer encountering your technology for the first time lacks this background. By following your instructions exactly as written, you surface hidden assumptions and create more comprehensive guidance. This validation also helps you experience the friction points developers will encounter, from awkward configuration steps to unclear error messages. These insights enable you to provide warnings, troubleshooting guidance, and reassurance exactly where developers need them most, creating documentation that truly serves its purpose.

Creating Code Examples That Work

Functional, accurate code examples are the cornerstone of effective technical documentation. They must work exactly as shown, or they risk undermining developer trust and slowing platform adoption. Common issues with ineffective code examples include

- Copy-paste errors that prevent code from running
- Context-dependent code that only works in specific environments
- Incomplete snippets missing crucial initializations or imports
- Out-of-date examples that fail with current versions

When examples fail, developers face a crisis of confidence. They can't easily determine if the issue stems from their environment, their understanding, or problems in your documentation. This uncertainty erodes trust in your entire platform.

To maintain quality and accuracy, follow these key practices:

- Ensure you're using validated code rather than writing examples directly in documentation.

- When possible, integrate examples into automated testing processes that validate against current versions.
- Ensure examples demonstrate proper error handling, naming conventions, and security practices.

Well-crafted examples do more than just demonstrate functionality—they serve as models of best practices in your ecosystem. By showing developers not just what works, but what works well, you help them build better applications while strengthening their trust in your platform.

Documentation Maintenance Systems That Scale

Documentation requires ongoing care and systematic processes as your technology evolves.

Establishing a Documentation Lifecycle

A well-defined documentation lifecycle ensures your content remains accurate and valuable over time. Here's how to implement one:

- Define review triggers (releases, API changes, deprecations).
- Establish clear ownership of documentation sections.
- Implement regular testing procedures.
- Create feedback channels for users.
- Conduct periodic content audits.

Documentation that falls out of sync with your technology erodes developer trust and increases support burden. To prevent this, integrate documentation into your product development cycle:

- Include documentation tasks in sprint planning.
- Assign clear owners to documentation updates.
- Track documentation changes alongside code changes.
- Make documentation updates part of the "definition of done" for feature changes.

This integration means treating documentation as a first-class citizen in your development process. Without this systematic approach, documentation quality inevitably declines as your product evolves. By contrast, documentation that evolves with your product builds trust and reduces support costs throughout the product lifecycle.

Managing Expanding Product Surfaces

As your platform grows, documentation complexity increases exponentially. Here's how to manage this growth effectively:

- Create modular content that can be updated independently.
- Develop templates for consistency.
- Implement version control to track changes.
- Automate code example validation.
- Establish clear ownership areas.

Documentation debt accumulates just like technical debt, with similarly damaging effects. When documentation lags behind product development, developers encounter frustrating mismatches between what's documented and what actually exists. This friction slows adoption, increases support costs, and damages trust in your platform.

Preventing documentation debt requires intentional architecture decisions that anticipate growth. Consider these key factors:

- Modular content with clear dependencies makes updates manageable.
- Consistent patterns reduce cognitive load for creators and consumers.
- Strategic structural choices determine scalability.
- Proper documentation architecture reduces long-term maintenance costs.

Maintaining high-quality documentation requires proactive integration into development workflows, scalable architecture, and responsive feedback systems. By prioritizing documentation efforts strategically and evolving content alongside your product, you foster trust, streamline support, and drive long-term platform success.

Using Feedback to Drive Improvements

Real-world developer feedback is the compass that guides documentation improvement. Implement structured feedback systems through

- Page-level feedback mechanisms
- Support channel monitoring
- Search term tracking
- Usage metrics analysis
- Periodic user testing with developers

A community forum question might highlight a common use case you never considered. These signals help you discover gaps that wouldn't be visible from within your organization.

Effective feedback systems combine both quantitative data (metrics, search patterns, usage statistics) and qualitative insights (support conversations, user testing, direct feedback). This balanced approach reveals not just what's happening (developers abandoning a specific tutorial) but why it's happening (outdated examples). Armed with this comprehensive understanding, you can focus your efforts on improvements that will have the greatest impact on developer success.

Content Prioritization Frameworks

Documentation resources are always limited, making strategic prioritization essential. The key is to evaluate content needs through a structured approach that ensures the most important documentation gets created first.

When prioritizing documentation efforts, consider these critical factors:

- **Criticality:** How important is this to core user journeys?
- **Usage patterns:** Which documentation paths are most frequently accessed?
- **Complexity:** How difficult is this feature to use without documentation?
- **Support impact:** What volume of support issues relate to this topic?
- **Strategic value:** How well does this align with business goals?

This systematic evaluation makes trade-offs explicit rather than implicit. While perfect documentation for everything isn't realistic, this approach ensures you're investing resources where they'll have the greatest impact. It replaces the reactive pattern of documenting whatever is newest or responding to the loudest complaints.

The most effective documentation strategy finds the sweet spot where developer needs and business objectives intersect. When you can address frequent pain points while supporting strategic initiatives, you create documentation that drives adoption and aligns with organizational goals—maximizing the return on your documentation investment.

DOCUMENTATION GAP ANALYSIS

A documentation gap analysis helps identify areas where your technical content needs improvement:

1. Map the developer journey for your technology by identifying the main paths developers take from first interest to mastery.
2. Audit your existing content by listing all pieces of documentation you currently provide.
3. Categorize each piece using the Diataxis framework, including tutorials, how-to guides, references, and explanations.
4. Mark gaps in your coverage by identifying journey stages that lack appropriate support.
5. Assess the quality of existing content by testing it against real-world developer use cases.
6. Create a prioritized list of documentation needs based on business impact and developer pain points.
7. Develop a documentation road map that addresses the highest priority gaps first.
8. Establish metrics to measure the effectiveness of your documentation improvements.

To systematize your documentation gap analysis, schedule regular reviews—quarterly or after major releases—and update your documentation road map accordingly. Be sure to assign clear ownership for follow-up actions and track progress using a shared checklist or project management tool to ensure continuous improvement.

Conclusion: The Craft of Technical Writing

Technical writing is both an art and a science, a craft that combines deep technical knowledge with empathy for the developer experience. The most effective technical writers don't just document features—they illuminate paths to success for developers at every stage of their journey.

By creating clear, accurate, and thoughtful content organized around the four core types, you don't just explain your technology—you enable developers to accomplish things they couldn't do before. Effective technical writing transforms your platform from a collection of features into a tool for developer success.

As you develop your technical writing practice, focus not just on what your technology does but on how developers experience it through your documentation. This empathetic perspective, combined with systematic maintenance processes, transforms technical writing from a reference resource into a powerful catalyst for developer success and sustainable competitive advantage for your platform.

The investment you make in structured, maintained documentation pays dividends throughout the developer journey. It accelerates onboarding, reduces support costs, encourages feature adoption, and builds trust in your platform. With developers having increasingly abundant choices, documentation quality can be the difference between a platform that thrives and one that struggles to gain traction. By approaching documentation as a system rather than a collection of documents, you create an asset that scales with your platform and sustains your developer community over time.

It's also worth noting that documentation is a complex and deep topic, one that you can build an entire career on. The goal of this chapter is to help you think of documentation in regard to its management and broader connection to Developer Relations.

CHAPTER 7

Maintaining High-Quality Documentation

Developer engagement sits at the intersection of technical credibility and relationship building. It's where your deep understanding of technology meets your ability to communicate, empathize, and build trust with developers. When done effectively, it creates a bridge between developer perspectives and your company's capabilities, transforming potential into success.

Authentic Developer Engagement

Developers can spot inauthenticity from a mile away. You've probably experienced those canned pitches that could have been directed at anyone. They don't work because authentic engagement isn't about perfecting a persona or brand—it's about bringing your genuine self to every interaction.

Building Your Authentic Voice

Finding your authentic voice means discovering the sweet spot where your personal strengths, genuine interests, and your company's needs overlap. Instead of creating a polished "professional" persona, focus on

1. Identifying your actual interests within your technology space
2. Recognizing your natural communication style rather than forcing someone else's
3. Acknowledging your unique background and how it shapes your perspective

K. Kemple, *Effective DevRel*, https://doi.org/10.1007/979-8-8688-2373-2_7

4. Sharing relevant personal experiences that relate to the developer journey
5. Being consistent in your values across different contexts

The magic happens when your enthusiasm aligns naturally with your company's direction. You're not forcing excitement or making claims you don't believe—you're sharing what genuinely matters to you. Developers respond to that authenticity because it's so rare.

Taking a Problem/Solution-First Approach

When engaging with developers, resist that urge to jump straight into your features. We've all experienced conversations where someone excitedly describes functionality we don't need while our attention drifts elsewhere. Instead

1. Ask probing questions about their use case and requirements
2. Understand their challenges before suggesting solutions
3. Frame your responses in terms of the problems they've identified
4. Match solution complexity to problem complexity—don't overcomplicate simple issues
5. Present options in order of relevance to their specific situation
6. Acknowledge the limitations of your proposed solutions honestly

This approach shows you're genuinely interested in solving their problems rather than just promoting your platform. It changes the entire dynamic from "let me tell you about us" to "let me understand you." The magic happens when a developer realizes you're actually listening—their body language shifts, they lean in, and suddenly you're having a real conversation instead of delivering a rehearsed pitch. This problem/solution approach not only builds trust but also empowers you to be an effective problem solver in your developer interactions.

Providing Clear Next Steps

Have you ever left a conversation feeling overwhelmed with information but completely unclear on what to do next? Many of us have experienced walking away from a booth or a meeting thinking, "That was interesting, but what am I supposed to do with it?"

Avoid creating this experience for developers. When wrapping up interactions

1. Provide one clear call to action (CTA) rather than multiple options
2. Ensure the next step is relevant to their expressed needs
3. Follow up when possible to ensure completion
4. Set proper expectations for support channels and response times

This focused approach dramatically increases the likelihood that developers will take action after your interaction. It transforms "That was an interesting chat" into "I'm actually going to try this."

Note At Slack, I had a developer approach me at a demo booth who was stuck testing his apps. His test org lacked the features he needed. I informed him about the sandbox environments we offer in our developer program, and I could have pointed him to our developer program signup page, which might seem like the logical CTA in this scenario.

Instead, I directed him to our docs on sandbox environments that covered everything from sign-up to creation to available features. This subtle shift made all the difference. Instead of just pointing to a default CTA, I showed him the direct path to solving his actual problem. This is the essence of effective developer engagement. Seeing past the obvious next step to what they truly need.

Sharing Relevant Resources

Generic resource recommendations rarely drive action. "Check out our documentation" is about as helpful as "Google it." Instead

1. Direct developers to specific documentation pages rather than general sections

2. Share code samples and tutorials that match their particular use case
3. Offer community resources when appropriate

Don't feel constrained by prepared demos or scripts. If a developer has a specific need, deviate from your standard flow to show them exactly what will help them most. That customized attention speaks volumes.

Building Technical Credibility

Let's be honest—technical credibility is your admission ticket to meaningful developer conversations. Without it, even your best engagement techniques will fall flat. But here's the good news: you don't need to be the world's foremost expert in everything. You just need sufficient depth to engage authentically and earn trust.

Depth vs. Breadth: Finding Your Balance

You'll constantly face this tension between going deep on a few technologies or maintaining broader knowledge across many areas. The right balance depends on your context:

- **Platform complexity:** More complex platforms often require deeper specialization.
- **Team size:** Smaller teams need broader knowledge; larger teams can support specialization.
- **Developer sophistication:** More advanced developer communities expect deeper expertise.
- **Platform maturity:** Newer platforms benefit from people who can connect to diverse ecosystems.

Rather than pursuing depth or breadth exclusively, aim for a "T-shaped" profile. This means maintaining broad knowledge across relevant technologies (the horizontal bar of the "T") while developing deep expertise in specific areas that genuinely interest you and align with your company's needs (the vertical bar of the "T"). This balance allows you to engage authentically and effectively with developers.

Continuous Learning Strategies

Technology evolves relentlessly, and maintaining credibility requires ongoing learning. But with a million demands on your time, how do you actually make this happen? Here are some specific strategies you can use to develop sustainable learning habits that fit within the constraints of your role:

1. **Dedicated learning time:** Block regular calendar time for hands-on exploration. Protect this time like you would an important meeting.
2. **Project-based learning:** Take on small, practical projects that force engagement with new aspects of your platform.
3. **Teaching as learning:** Commit to creating content on topics that stretch your knowledge. Nothing reveals gaps like having to explain something.
4. **Internal knowledge sharing:** Establish regular exchanges with product and engineering teams to stay current.

The most valuable learning happens at the edges of your comfort zone—where you have enough foundation to build upon but are stretching into new territory. Keep a personal development journal that tracks your learning journey and celebrates your progress.

Getting Hands-On with the Product

The honest truth? Without intentional practice, your technical skills will atrophy while you're busy with presentations, content creation, and meetings. Consider these approaches to keep your technical edge:

1. Maintain a personal development environment for your product where you can experiment freely.
2. Create working examples rather than theoretical explanations.
3. Participate in internal hackathons or engineering initiatives.
4. Join product discovery sessions to understand what teams are building.

5. Use your products for actual tasks whenever possible.
6. Build side-projects that utilize your platform.

These practices don't just maintain your skills—they generate practical examples and insights that strengthen and make your engagement work more relevant.

Asking Effectively

In developer engagement, you're constantly asking developers to try features, share feedback, participate in beta programs, or contribute to discussions. How you make these requests dramatically impacts whether they take action or politely smile and forget about you 30 seconds later.

The Psychology of Asking Developers

Understanding what drives developers to say yes (or no) to requests transforms your effectiveness:

1. **Autonomy:** Developers resist feeling manipulated or forced into actions.
2. **Mastery:** They respond positively to opportunities that utilize their technical skills.
3. **Purpose:** They engage when they see meaningful impact beyond marketing goals.
4. **Reciprocity:** They respond to mutual value exchange rather than one-sided requests.
5. **Recognition:** They appreciate acknowledgment of their specific expertise and contributions.

When you integrate these principles into how you frame requests to developers, you dramatically increase the likelihood of positive responses and meaningful engagement.

The Three Rs Framework

When asking for participation, cooperation, or support, follow the Three Rs framework:

- **Recognition:** Acknowledge why you're asking this specific person, recognizing their unique expertise or perspective.
- **Request:** Clearly state what you're asking for, including the scope of commitment.
- **Reward:** Explain the value the person will receive from participating, whether that's visibility, learning, connection, or other benefits.

This framework ensures that requests create mutual value rather than one-sided transactions, building sustainable relationships instead of exhausting goodwill.

Common Developer Asking Mistakes

Watch for these common pitfalls when making requests to developers:

- **Assumptive gratitude:** Thanking developers preemptively before they've agreed. ("Thanks in advance for testing our API!")
- **Vague scope:** Failing to specify the time commitment or technical environment required. ("Could you try our new feature sometime?")
- **Benefit ambiguity:** Not clearly articulating what's in it for them beyond helping you.
- **Last-minute pressure:** Making requests without adequate lead time for busy developers.
- **Generic requests:** Failing to personalize the ask to their specific interests or expertise.

These mistakes significantly reduce your success rate and can damage your credibility with the developer community. Developers quickly tune out people who repeatedly make low-quality requests.

Sustainable Engagement Practices

The brutal truth about developer engagement? It can consume every waking hour if you let it. Work can quickly become boundless when it involves building relationships, creating content, providing feedback, and supporting developers across multiple channels. Without intentional management, your calendar fills with endless requests and commitments.

Recognizing the Warning Signs of Burnout

Burnout doesn't arrive suddenly with a dramatic crash. It develops gradually through a predictable pattern:

- **Enthusiasm:** Initial excitement about making an impact
- **Stagnation:** Realizing the scope of demands exceeds capacity
- **Frustration:** Feeling unable to meet expectations or make progress
- **Apathy:** Disengaging to protect remaining energy
- **Crisis:** Reaching physical, mental, or emotional breaking points

In developer engagement, watch for warning signs like dreading interactions you once enjoyed, procrastinating on content creation, feeling resentful about engagement expectations, or experiencing anxiety about keeping up with technical changes. The sooner you recognize these patterns, the easier they are to address.

Building Sustainable Routines

To maintain energy and effectiveness, establish intentional routines that preserve your resources:

- **Calendar blocking:** Reserve specific time blocks for deep work, content creation, and recovery. Protect these blocks as fiercely as you would external commitments.
- **Travel boundaries:** Set clear limits on days away per month or quarter. Even enthusiastic travelers experience diminishing returns when traveling too frequently.

- **Platform boundaries:** Define when and how you engage with communication channels. Continuous availability across all platforms leads to fragmented attention and exhaustion.
- **Energy auditing:** Regularly assess which activities energize you and which drain you. Restructure your approach to maximize energizing work while managing necessary but draining tasks.
- **Prioritization systems:** Develop frameworks for evaluating opportunities and requests. Not all activities deserve equal time, even if they seem valuable in isolation.
- **Recovery rituals:** Establish consistent practices that help you recharge. Whether it's exercise, creative pursuits, or disconnected time, these practices are essential professional investments, not optional luxuries.

These routines create the foundation for sustainable performance, preventing the all-too-common cycle of heroic sprints followed by prolonged recovery periods.

Setting Expectations and Boundaries

Clear expectations and boundaries are essential for sustainable engagement:

- **With managers:** Have explicit conversations about priorities, travel expectations, and availability requirements. Revisit these regularly as organizational needs evolve.
- **With developers:** Establish transparent patterns for engagement, response times, and appropriate channels. Consistency builds trust while preventing unrealistic expectations.
- **With yourself:** Acknowledge your own limitations. Perfectionism and unrealistic self-expectations often drive burnout as much as external demands.
- **With your team:** Develop a shared understanding of capacity and coverage. Creating mutual support systems prevents individual overload while ensuring developer needs are met.

By proactively setting and communicating these boundaries, you create the conditions for long-term effectiveness rather than short-term heroics.

Managing the Emotional Load

Developer engagement involves significant emotional labor. Maintaining enthusiasm, navigating conflicts, and managing relationships across many contexts takes real energy. To sustain this work

- Recognize emotional labor as real work that consumes energy.
- Build in recovery time after high-intensity interactions.
- Create support networks with others who understand the challenges.
- Practice appropriate professional detachment without losing authenticity.
- Develop personal renewal practices that restore your emotional energy.

The goal isn't to eliminate emotional engagement—that would undermine authentic work. It's about making that engagement sustainable through intentional management.

CREATING YOUR ENGAGEMENT PLAYBOOK

Take time to develop your personal engagement strategy by working through these key elements:

- Document your engagement channels by listing all platforms where you interact with developers and noting the primary purpose of each.
- Map your expertise areas by creating a skills matrix showing your technical depth across different domains.
- Define response protocols by establishing guidelines for how quickly and thoroughly you'll respond in different situations.
- Create content templates by developing reusable formats for common content types like tutorials, announcements, and technical deep dives.
- Set measurement criteria by determining how you'll track the success of different engagement activities.
- Establish bandwidth management practices by defining clear boundaries for your time, attention, and commitments.

- Design a learning road map that identifies technologies you need to master and creates a plan for building that expertise.
- Create a personal feedback system to track which engagement approaches are most effective with your developer audience.

Review and update your playbook quarterly to ensure it evolves with your role and developer needs. This living document will help you maintain focus, consistency, and sustainability in your engagement efforts.

Conclusion: Building Bridges Through Engagement

Effective developer engagement creates bridges between technical capabilities and real-world solutions. By combining deep technical knowledge with authentic communication and structured engagement practices, you transform from a spokesperson into a trusted guide helping developers navigate complex technical landscapes.

The approaches outlined in this chapter—authentic voice, demonstrated technical credibility, practical engagement techniques, effective asking, and sustainable practices—provide a foundation for meaningful developer relationships. These relationships enable you to gather valuable insights, influence product direction, and ultimately help more developers succeed with your technology.

Remember that sustainable engagement is a marathon, not a sprint. By implementing the boundaries, routines, and practices we've discussed, you can create a long-term impact without burning out. Your effectiveness ultimately comes from balancing technical depth, authentic communication, and personal sustainability—creating value for developers, your company, and yourself.

CHAPTER 8

Turning Feedback into Priorities

I bet this sounds familiar. You're on that video call with the product team, excited to share feedback from developers. You've carefully prepared everything, complete with a solid solution to the problem. When you present it, everyone seems interested. They nod along. They ask questions. Success, right?

Then comes the familiar letdown. "This is great feedback, but we're focused on our current road map. Let's revisit this next quarter." The call ends, and you're left wondering why such important feedback keeps getting postponed.

We often blame product teams for not prioritizing our feedback. However, the real problem might be in how we present that feedback. Random developer comments rarely drive change, but consolidated evidence and business impact almost always do.

This chapter will help you transform scattered developer experiences into compelling evidence that drives real product improvements. You'll learn systematic approaches to gathering feedback, frameworks for prioritizing issues, and techniques for presenting findings in ways that align with business goals. When you master these skills, your feedback becomes impossible to ignore.

Setting Up Journey Audits That Capture Meaningful Data

Most developer feedback lacks context. Developers might tell you something's confusing, but they rarely explain exactly why they got stuck or what they were trying to accomplish. Journey audits fill these gaps by systematically documenting how developers experience specific workflows within your platform.

K. Kemple, *Effective DevRel*, https://doi.org/10.1007/979-8-8688-2373-2_8

The Journey Audit Process

A journey audit examines a specific developer workflow, typically related to an important milestone like creating a first application or deploying to production. Unlike random testing, journey audits follow a structured methodology:

1. Define clear personas and scenarios for specific developer types and their goals.
2. Map the expected journey these personas would follow for the particular workflow.
3. Experience the journey firsthand by stepping through every interaction.
4. Document observations systematically using consistent formats.
5. Identify patterns across different journeys.
6. Prioritize findings based on impact severity and business alignment.

This systematic approach transforms subjective impressions into objective observations that drive action. When you bring concrete, well-documented findings to stakeholders, you change the conversation from opinions to evidence.

Structuring Journey Audits for Maximum Impact

For journey audits to drive meaningful change, they must be conducted with intention and rigor. Here are the key elements of an effective journey audit program:

- **Regular cadence:** Schedule journey audits on a predictable calendar—quarterly for core experiences, monthly for rapidly evolving areas, and immediately after significant releases.
- **Fresh perspectives:** Rotate team members through audit responsibilities and occasionally bring in people outside the immediate team to catch issues that insiders might overlook.
- **Comprehensive coverage:** Ensure your audit program examines all critical paths, not just the happy paths or most common scenarios. Pay special attention to first-time experiences, cross-platform transitions, integration with external systems, and error recovery scenarios.

- **Comparative analysis:** Track changes over time by comparing audit results with previous findings. This highlights both improvements and regressions while demonstrating progress on known issues.

Journey audits aren't just about finding problems. They build your credibility when advocating for developers. When you come to the table with systematically gathered evidence rather than anecdotes, product teams take your feedback seriously.

Creating Friction Logs That Drive Product Improvements

While journey audits provide a holistic assessment, friction logs offer detailed documentation of developers' challenges. These structured records transform vague frustrations into actionable evidence.

Anatomy of an Effective Friction Log

A friction log is a detailed record of a specific developer experience that captures both the objective steps and the subjective impressions. Effective friction logs include several key components:

- Contextual information
  - Date and time of the experience
  - Environmental details (OS, browser, device, etc.)
  - Developer profile (experience level, role, etc.)
  - Goal or task being attempted
  - Starting point and expected outcome
- Step-by-step documentation
  - Each action taken, listed sequentially
  - Expected result at each step
  - Actual result observed
  - Time spent on challenging steps
  - Screenshots or videos capturing the experience

- Qualitative assessment
    - Points of confusion or uncertainty
    - Emotional response at key moments
    - Questions that arose during the process
    - Workarounds attempted
    - Specific suggestions for improvement
- Severity classification
    - Impact on task completion (blocked, delayed, irritated)
    - Likelihood of affecting other developers
    - Relationship to critical user journeys
    - Technical complexity of the issue

This comprehensive structure ensures that friction logs contain all the information needed to reproduce issues, understand their impact, and develop appropriate solutions (see Appendix K).

From Individual Experiences to Systematic Understanding

While individual friction logs provide valuable snapshots, their true power emerges when analyzed collectively. Implement processes to extract patterns from multiple logs:

- Create a categorization system with tags by feature area, journey stage, severity, and impact type.
- Build a central repository that's searchable and filterable, accessible to all relevant teams.
- Schedule regular analysis sessions monthly to identify recurring themes.
- Develop quantification methods to track the frequency of issue types, severity trends, and time impact.

These processes transform individual experiences into compelling evidence of systematic issues and opportunities. Even highly subjective feedback becomes actionable when patterns emerge across multiple developers encountering similar challenges.

Practical Frameworks for Organizing and Prioritizing Feedback

I've seen so many DevRel teams drown in feedback without making progress. They collect mountains of data, carefully document every issue, and then... nothing happens. The insights sit in documents, the developers keep experiencing the same problems, and everyone gets frustrated.

The key to breaking this cycle is having structured frameworks for turning raw feedback into prioritized actions. These frameworks create clarity when you're facing dozens or hundreds of potential issues. They help you focus resources where they'll have the greatest impact and build credibility with both developers and internal teams.

Note Over the course of multiple hackathons, developer conversations, and partner feedback sessions, I kept encountering the same pattern: developers were confused about whether to build a "Slack app," an "AI app," a "workflow app," or install a "connector." Partners like Wrangle were managing separate apps and connectors with authentication nightmares. Admins were struggling with fragmented management across different integration types.

Rather than treating these as isolated complaints, I systematically documented the friction across all personas—developers, admins, end users, and partners. I quantified the impact: teams using the platform grew 35% more month-over-month, but adoption friction from this confusion was holding us back. I connected it to strategic priorities: our V2MOM goal to increase users deriving value from apps and workflows, and our product principles of "don't make me think" and "be a great host."

The result? We changed our entire platform strategy. The consolidated evidence made it impossible to ignore: every workflow, every AI feature, every connector—they were all apps underneath. The artificial boundaries we'd created were the problem. This feedback-driven case led to a fundamental shift in how we position and build the Slack platform.

Building the Feedback-to-Action Pipeline

A feedback-to-action pipeline creates a clear path from developer frustrations to product improvements. This pipeline doesn't just ensure that feedback gets addressed. It builds developer trust by demonstrating that you value their input and take action based on what you hear.

The pipeline consists of seven key stages:

1. **Collection and documentation:** Gather feedback through journey audits, friction logs, support channels, community forums, and direct conversations. Use consistent formats to capture what matters.

2. **Categorization and prioritization:** Sort feedback by affected area, severity, strategic alignment, and potential impact. Group related items to identify patterns rather than treating each piece in isolation.

3. **Analysis and synthesis:** Identify patterns, root causes, and potential solutions. Look beyond symptoms to understand underlying issues that might affect multiple experiences.

4. **Stakeholder alignment:** Build consensus with product and engineering teams on the importance of issues and the approach to addressing them. Bring data and evidence rather than just opinions.

5. **Implementation tracking:** Monitor progress from acknowledgment through resolution. Keep records of how long issues take to address and what barriers emerge.

6. **Outcome validation:** Verify that changes resolve the original issues through follow-up testing. Don't assume that implemented solutions actually fixed the problems they targeted.

7. **Community communication:** Close the loop by informing developers about improvements based on their feedback. Show them that their input matters.

This pipeline converts developer input into platform improvements through a clear sequence of stages. By maintaining this structured approach, you ensure feedback doesn't just disappear into a void but drives real platform enhancements.

From Anecdotes to Evidence

The transition from collection to action often stalls because feedback appears anecdotal or subjective. To overcome this challenge, build compelling cases by transforming individual observations into persuasive evidence:

- Quantify impact
    - How many developers likely encounter this issue?
    - How much time does it waste per occurrence?
    - What percentage of affected developers abandon their efforts?
    - How does this friction affect critical business metrics like activation or retention?
- Connect to strategic priorities
    - How does this issue affect developer adoption?
    - What impact does it have on platform expansion?
    - How does it influence developer satisfaction and advocacy?
    - Does it create a competitive disadvantage or opportunity?
- Provide contextual comparison
    - How do competitors handle similar scenarios?
    - How does this experience compare to industry best practices?
    - Has this approach been successful in analogous contexts?

These techniques help transform individual feedback into compelling evidence by combining metrics, strategic alignment, and comparative analysis. This data-driven approach creates clear narratives that demonstrate urgency and motivate stakeholders to address developer pain points.

The RICE Prioritization Framework

Not all feedback can or should be addressed immediately. Effective prioritization ensures you focus on the issues that will create the most value for developers and your business.

The RICE framework uses four factors to determine priority:

1. **Reach:** How many developers does this issue affect?
    a. **High:** Impacts most developers using the platform
    b. **Medium:** Affects a significant segment or key persona
    c. **Low:** Impacts a small, specific subset of developers
2. **Impact:** How significantly does this issue affect developer success?
    a. **High:** Blocks completion of critical tasks
    b. **Medium:** Creates significant friction but has workarounds
    c. **Low:** Minor annoyance that doesn't prevent progress
3. **Confidence:** How certain are we about the scope and impact of this issue?
    a. **High:** Consistently reproduced with clear documentation
    b. **Medium:** Reported by multiple sources but with some variation
    c. **Low:** Limited observation or inconsistent reproduction
4. **Effort:** How much work would be required to address this issue?
    a. **High:** Requires significant engineering or cross-team coordination
    b. **Medium:** Needs moderate investment but within a single team's scope
    c. **Low:** Can be resolved with minimal resources

By assigning numeric values to each dimension and calculating a RICE score (Reach × Impact × Confidence / Effort), you create an objective basis for comparing different feedback items. This approach helps you focus on high-value opportunities that maximize return on investment.

The Impact-Effort Matrix

Another effective framework is the Impact-Effort Matrix, which plots feedback items on two axes:

1. **Impact:** Effect on developer experience and business outcomes (vertical axis)
2. **Effort:** Resources required to implement the solution (horizontal axis)

This visual approach identifies four categories of feedback:

- **Quick Wins (High Impact, Low Effort):** Implement immediately.
    - These create substantial value with minimal investment.
    - Should be your top priority for immediate action.
- **Major Projects (High Impact, High Effort):** Require careful planning.
    - These deserve significant resources.
    - Need thoughtful project management and stakeholder alignment.
- **Fill-Ins (Low Impact, Low Effort):** Address when resources allow.
    - While not transformative, these can accumulate to improve the overall experience.
    - Good opportunities for new team members or slack time.
- **Thankless Tasks (Low Impact, High Effort):** Reconsider or defer.
    - These rarely justify their cost.
    - Should be the lowest priority unless evidence changes.

These frameworks transform subjective opinions into structured decisions, making feedback prioritization more transparent and defensible.

Implementing Feedback Loops That Build Developer Trust

I've seen too many companies ask developers for feedback only to ghost them. The developers never hear back, never see improvements based on their input, and eventually stop bothering to share their experiences. It's a trust-killer.

Creating closed-loop feedback systems completely changes this dynamic. When developers see their input translated into real improvements, they become invested in your platform's success. They provide more detailed feedback, contribute suggestions more readily, and become advocates for your technology.

Designing Transparent Feedback Systems

Transparency builds trust. When developers can see what happens with their feedback, they're more likely to provide more in the future. Implement these transparency mechanisms:

- Public issue trackers that show the status of known issues
- Regular feedback summaries highlighting patterns and planned actions
- Clear expectations about what feedback will and won't be addressed
- Acknowledgment processes for all feedback, even when action isn't immediate

These transparency mechanisms transform feedback from a black hole into a visible process that developers can track and understand. When developers see others encountering similar issues and those issues being addressed, it validates their experiences and builds confidence in your platform.

Closing the Loop with Developers

The final step in effective feedback is communicating back to the developer community. This communication builds trust and encourages continued feedback:

- Acknowledge contributions by thanking developers who provide valuable feedback.
- Provide status updates about issues they've raised, even when solutions aren't immediate.

- Explain decisions when feedback can't be addressed, sharing the constraints.
- Celebrate improvements by highlighting the connection between developer input and product evolution.

These communication practices transform feedback from a one-time transaction into an ongoing dialogue that strengthens relationships while continuously improving your platform.

Building Developer Confidence Through Feedback

When done well, feedback systems do more than improve your product. They transform how developers perceive your platform and company. Each time you acknowledge, address, and communicate about feedback, you send a powerful message: "We're listening, we care, and we're committed to your success."

This commitment builds a foundation of trust that extends beyond any individual interaction. Developers become more willing to try new features, forgive occasional issues, and advocate for your platform. They know that if problems arise, there's a reliable path to resolution.

Systematically collecting, prioritizing, and acting on feedback creates a virtuous cycle. As developers see improvements based on their input, they provide more thoughtful feedback. As feedback quality improves, so does your ability to make meaningful enhancements. This upward spiral continuously improves both your platform and your relationship with the developer community.

DESIGNING YOUR FEEDBACK FRAMEWORK

Apply the concepts from this chapter by creating your own feedback system. Work through these steps to establish a structured approach to gathering and acting on developer feedback:

1. Create a basic journey audit framework for your platform by listing two to three critical developer journeys to audit, defining success criteria for each journey, creating a schedule for regular audits, and identifying team members to participate in the process.

2. Customize the friction log template for your needs by adapting the template sections to match your platform's specific requirements, creating guidelines for severity classification, defining your documentation standards, and establishing your repository for storing and organizing logs.
3. Design your feedback-to-action workflow by mapping out your process for routing feedback to appropriate teams, creating prioritization criteria, defining your tracking system for feedback implementation, and establishing communication channels for status updates.
4. Build your analysis framework by choosing key metrics to track, creating categorization tags, setting up regular review sessions, and defining reporting templates.
5. Implement a feedback loop mechanism by designing a process for acknowledging feedback, creating templates for status updates, establishing criteria for when and how to communicate decisions, and developing channels for sharing improvements based on feedback.
6. Create a prioritization framework by defining your RICE criteria or Impact-Effort matrix, establishing scoring guidelines, developing a review process for evaluating feedback, and determining how often you'll reassess priorities.
7. Test your framework with a small pilot by selecting one developer journey to audit, creating friction logs for that journey, analyzing the results with your new framework, and refining your approach based on what you learn.
8. Document your approach so that other team members can participate consistently in the feedback process.

After completing the exercise, schedule regular review sessions to monitor progress and update your frameworks. Assign clear ownership for follow-ups, and document each step so the process becomes repeatable and easily scalable as your team grows.

Conclusion: Transforming Feedback into Meaningful Action

You've likely experienced the frustration of valuable feedback disappearing into the void. The frameworks we've explored in this chapter give you the tools to break that pattern and turn developer insights into real platform improvements.

Journey audits give you the context to understand developer experiences deeply. Friction logs provide the structure to document issues comprehensively. Prioritization frameworks like RICE and Impact-Effort help you focus on what matters most. Feedback-to-action pipelines create clear paths from observation to resolution. Transparent communication builds trust and keeps developers engaged.

The magic happens when these elements work together as a system. What starts as a scattered collection of complaints transforms into structured evidence that drives priorities. Those priorities become improvements that make developers' lives better. And those improvements build the trust that makes your platform stand out in developers' minds.

As you build your feedback system, remember that perfection isn't the goal. Start small, focusing on one critical developer journey. Document the friction points systematically. Prioritize the issues that affect the most developers. Implement the changes that offer the biggest return on investment. And always, always close the loop by letting developers know their input made a difference.

The consistency of this process, more than any individual improvement, is what ultimately builds developer trust and advocacy. When developers know you're genuinely listening and acting on what you hear, they become more than users of your platform. They become partners in making it better.

PART III

Driving Business Impact

CHAPTER 9

Transitioning from Doer to Leader

If you've ever felt caught in an endless cycle of creating content and attending events without seeing clear results, you're not alone. Many DevRel professionals find themselves in a reactionary state, always having to adjust tactics or explain what they do and why it matters.

Note It was 2021 at Apollo GraphQL, and on paper, we were crushing it—podcast appearances and live streams launching weekly, conference talks booked solid, workshops scheduled back-to-back. Then I looked at my calendar: three hours of program management for every one hour actually talking to developers. My team had become project managers of their own initiatives. We'd created what I later labeled YAP, or "Yet Another Program" (which we'll cover in Chapter 11). The wake-up call came when I couldn't remember the last time I'd done a deep-dive friction log. We were everywhere and nowhere at once—busy, but not as effective as we could be.

This chapter will help you move beyond "random acts of DevRel" by developing purposeful strategies that create lasting impact for developers and your organization. We'll explore how to evolve from an individual contributor to a strategic leader, build meaningful relationships across your organization, and create the conditions for sustained DevRel success.

K. Kemple, *Effective DevRel*, https://doi.org/10.1007/979-8-8688-2373-2_9

From Individual Contributor to DevRel Leader

Most DevRel professionals start as individual contributors. They're advocates, technical writers, program managers, or developer experience engineers. Maybe you can see yourself in one of those roles right now. You've been crushing it, connecting with developers, creating valuable content, organizing killer events, or building tools that make developers' lives easier.

Then, one day, someone taps you on the shoulder and says, "Hey, how would you like to lead the team?" And just like that, everything changes.

Here's the truth, though. The skills that make you an excellent IC aren't necessarily the same ones that make you an effective leader. It's like being good at playing an instrument and suddenly being asked to conduct the entire orchestra—it's an entirely different set of requirements.

Mindset Shift

As a successful individual contributor, you're valued for your output—the content you create, the code you write, and the developers you help. I remember being so proud of my own output—the blog posts with my name on them, the talks I gave, and the developers who reached out to thank me personally. It felt good, you know?

Leadership requires a fundamental mindset shift:

- Doing everything yourself → Enabling others to succeed
- Personal productivity → Team effectiveness
- Technical expertise → Strategic vision
- Immediate results → Long-term impact

This shift can feel uncomfortable at first. You might think, "I could write that blog post faster myself," or "It would be quicker if I just handled this developer's issue." That's normal! However, authentic leadership means optimizing for scale and sustainability rather than short-term efficiency.

Building Systems, Not Just Solutions

Individual contributors solve specific problems; leaders build systems that solve whole categories of problems. As you transition to leadership, focus on

- Creating frameworks that allow your team to make consistent, aligned decisions.
- Establishing processes that reduce friction and increase effectiveness.
- Developing templates that accelerate work without sacrificing quality.
- Building measurement systems that demonstrate impact and guide improvement.

For example, instead of writing individual blog posts, design a content strategy framework that guides topic selection, provides templates, establishes quality standards, and measures effectiveness. This approach multiplies your impact far beyond what you could accomplish personally.

From Team Player to Strategic Partner

When you're an individual contributor, you're focused on execution within your immediate sphere. You're heads down, creating content, talking to developers, writing docs, and organizing events. But when you step into leadership, your gaze must lift up and out.

As a leader, you need to expand your focus to include business strategy, organizational dynamics, and cross-functional relationships:

- Understand business priorities beyond your immediate team.
- Connect DevRel activities to organizational objectives.
- Identify strategic leverage points where DevRel can drive a disproportionate impact.
- Build relationships with leaders across functions.
- Communicate value in terms that resonate with different stakeholders.

This transition shifts your perspective from executing specific tasks to orchestrating systems that create a broader impact. You're no longer just contributing to the value cycle. You're designing it.

The Great Distancing: A Historical Pitfall

There's this fascinating bit of DevRel history I like to call "The Great Distancing" that still echoes through our work today. You know how it goes. Developers have this legendary skepticism toward traditional marketing. They can smell inauthentic messaging from a mile away. So naturally, as the field of DevRel emerged, many practitioners (myself included, if I'm being honest) went out of their way to establish their identity as "definitely not marketing."

"No, no, we're not trying to sell you anything! We're developers just like you!"

This positioning made sense at the time. It helped build credibility and trust with technical audiences who'd grown weary of being targeted by marketing tactics that didn't speak their language. I still remember the relief on developers' faces when they realized I understood their technical challenges and wasn't just there to push a product.

But here's the thing about defining yourself by what you're not. You can accidentally create a whole new set of problems. Over time, this distancing became a pitfall for many teams, including some I've led:

- We'd reinvent processes from scratch instead of adapting perfectly good marketing methodologies because we were allergic to anything that felt too "marketing-ish."
- We'd resist measuring our impact in business terms because that's what "those marketing people" did.
- Our execution would be inconsistent because we'd rejected program management approaches that could have helped us.
- And we'd isolate ourselves from the teams we needed as allies.

I've sat in too many meetings where I've heard DevRel folks basically position themselves as "the anti-marketing marketing team" and then struggle to articulate their strategic value. It's one of those historical patterns we have to recognize before we can escape it.

Avoiding "Random Acts of DevRel"

DevRel teams often fall into the trap of activity-oriented work—creating content, attending events, building demos, and engaging with developers without clearly understanding how these activities connect to broader objectives. This reactive approach emerges from several underlying factors:

- **Identity-based resistance:** When DevRel teams define themselves primarily in opposition to marketing and sales, they often reject strategic approaches associated with those functions, even when those approaches enhance their effectiveness.
- **Unclear business alignment:** When DevRel teams lack visibility into company priorities or aren't included in strategic planning, they default to general-purpose activities that seem universally valuable.
- **Measurement by activity:** Teams that have rejected outcome-oriented metrics often use output metrics (number of blog posts, event attendance, repository stars) rather than measuring actual impact.
- **Request-driven priorities:** Without a strategic framework for evaluation, DevRel teams often respond to the loudest voices or most recent requests rather than focusing on the highest-value opportunities.

Recognizing these pitfalls is the first step toward meaningful change. By understanding how activity-driven habits take root, DevRel teams can shift their focus from reactive execution to intentional, strategic impact. This transition requires not only clarity of purpose but also a willingness to rethink established patterns and connect everyday work to long-term goals.

Symptoms of Random Acts of DevRel

These underlying factors reveal clear warning signs that your team may be caught in a cycle of random, disconnected activities:

- **Difficulty explaining impact:** Team members struggle to articulate how their work contributes to company success beyond vague references to "awareness" or "developer engagement."
- **Reactive calendar:** The team's road map consists primarily of responding to events, requests, and opportunities rather than proactively driving strategic initiatives.

- **Measurement gaps:** Success metrics focus on activities (content produced, events attended) rather than outcomes that matter to developers and the business.
- **Burnout cycles:** Team members experience periods of intense activity followed by exhaustion, with little sense of progress toward meaningful goals.
- **Budget vulnerability:** DevRel faces disproportionate scrutiny during resource constraints because its connection to business outcomes isn't clearly established.

These symptoms highlight why it's so important to pause and reassess. If left unchecked, a cycle of random activities can undermine both team morale and organizational trust, making it difficult to secure ongoing support. Breaking free from this pattern starts with acknowledging its presence and preparing to approach DevRel work in a more deliberate, goal-oriented way.

Note [INSERT ANECDOTE: Experience of leading a team that was constantly racing from event to event with no strategic direction, resulting in burnout and budget cuts]

Creating Your Strategic Road Map

Strategic DevRel doesn't mean abandoning tactical activities. Content creation, event participation, and developer engagement remain essential. The difference lies in how you select, design, combine, and measure these activities with intentional purpose.

Thinking Future-Back for Program Development

Look at most DevRel road maps, and you'll spot a pattern. They start with whatever the team is doing, then sprinkle in new stuff they want to try. It's like adding rooms to a house without looking at the blueprint. Before you know it, you've got a kitchen in the attic and a bathroom in the garage.

Strategic program development flips this approach on its head and works future-back instead:

- **Define the desired future state:** What specific business and developer outcomes do you want to achieve in 12–18 months?
- **Identify key enabling conditions:** What must happen for those outcomes to occur?
- **Map critical capabilities:** What DevRel capabilities are essential to create those conditions?
- **Design coherent programs:** What ongoing programmatic activities will build and apply those capabilities?
- **Establish progress indicators:** How will you measure movement toward the desired future state?

This future-back approach ensures that programs connect directly to strategic outcomes rather than merely continuing or incrementing existing activities.

Anatomy of a Strategic DevRel Program

So, what makes a DevRel program truly strategic instead of just a bunch of random activities? It's not about doing different things. It's about doing things differently. Strategic DevRel programs share several key characteristics:

- **Clear outcome definition:** The program has measurable outcomes tied to developer success and business objectives. You know exactly what needle you're trying to move.
- **Coherent components:** Individual activities within the program connect logically to each other and the defined outcomes. Your webinar series, documentation improvements, and sample apps all work together toward the same goal rather than feeling like separate projects.
- **Sustainability model:** The program includes mechanisms for ongoing operation without continuous heroic effort from the team. No more 3 a.m. coffee-fueled coding sessions before every demo day.
- **Evolution path:** The program has defined stages of maturity with associated capability requirements and success metrics. You can see how it will grow and evolve over time.

- **Resource scaling:** As the program demonstrates value, explicit models exist to expand its impact with additional resources. "If we had one more person, here's exactly how we'd scale this."
- **Cross-functional integration:** The program clearly defines how it connects to adjacent functions like Product, Marketing, and Engineering. Everyone understands their role in making it successful.

By building programs with these characteristics, you create a foundation for long-term impact and continuous improvement rather than executing disconnected tactical efforts that leave everyone exhausted with little to show for it.

Managing Up: Building Executive Relationships

Success in DevRel requires more than just executing programs—it demands building understanding and support across the entire organization, particularly with executive leadership. Your mission is to help every executive understand DevRel's purpose and value in terms that resonate with their priorities.

Building Organization-Wide Support

DevRel programs are often launched with strong intentions but can fall short without organization-wide support, leading to scattered activities that lack true alignment with business goals. To achieve meaningful impact and sustained value, it's essential to move beyond isolated efforts and foster broad advocacy across the company:

- **Create clear messaging:** Develop a consistent narrative about DevRel's role and impact that resonates with different departments. Focus on how DevRel supports their specific goals and challenges.
- **Share success stories:** Tailor your communications to resonate with different stakeholders by focusing on their priorities and concerns. Share relevant metrics, case studies, and success stories demonstrating DevRel's impact on each department's objectives and goals.
- **Engage meaningfully:** Participate in product and project discussions, join company calls, and ask questions when needed.

A well-understood DevRel function is well-supported. By helping others understand your team's purpose and impact, you create advocates who will champion your initiatives and provide the resources needed to serve developers effectively.

Building Strategic Influence

DevRel functions typically lack direct authority over many areas that affect developer experience, making strategic influence essential:

- **Cultivate executive relationships:** Develop connections with leaders across the organization based on delivering value and addressing their priorities.
- **Build data-driven narratives:** Use quantitative and qualitative evidence to create compelling cases for developer experience investments.
- **Create visibility into developer impact:** Implement systems that make developer success and challenges visible throughout the organization.
- **Leverage external perspective:** Use competitive comparisons, industry benchmarks, and market analysis to provide context for internal decisions.
- **Develop internal champions:** Identify and support advocates for developer experience across different organizational functions.

This influence strategy enables DevRel leaders to shape decisions and priorities far beyond their direct scope of control.

Communicating Effectively

Beyond demonstrating business value, effective DevRel leaders develop communication approaches tailored to different stakeholders and situations.

When communicating with executives, be sure to apply the following best practices:

- Focus on business outcomes first, activities second.
- Present information in concise, visually oriented formats.
- Connect DevRel initiatives to strategic company priorities.

- Use stories that illustrate key points with concrete examples.
- Anticipate and address potential concerns proactively.
- Offer clear next steps and decision points when needed.

When trying to gain cross-functional leadership support, your communication style should

- Emphasize shared goals and mutual benefits
- Acknowledge constraints and competing priorities
- Propose collaborative approaches rather than competing demands
- Demonstrate an understanding of their functional priorities
- Support requests with data relevant to their objectives
- Build ongoing relationships outside of specific request contexts

By mastering these communication strategies, DevRel leaders not only secure vital support but also foster a culture of collaboration and trust across the organization. This foundation paves the way for driving impactful change and building the resilience necessary for future growth.

Creating a Learning Culture within DevRel

In a field evolving as rapidly as Developer Relations, creating a learning culture isn't just beneficial—it's essential for long-term effectiveness. As a strategic leader, you're responsible for building an environment where continuous learning is both expected and enabled.

Balancing Immediate Delivery with Long-Term Growth

DevRel teams are now facing constant pressure to deliver results. It's easy to postpone learning and development in favor of immediate outputs. However, this approach leads to stagnation and diminishing effectiveness over time.

Strategic leaders intentionally balance short-term delivery with long-term capability building:

- **Allocate protected learning time:** Designate specific time blocks for skill development, experimentation, and exploration. Defend this time when delivery pressures mount.
- **Connect learning to application:** Create opportunities to immediately apply new knowledge to current challenges, reinforcing the value of learning.
- **Celebrate growth milestones:** Recognize and reward learning achievements alongside delivery metrics, signaling their importance to the team.
- **Model continuous learning:** Demonstrate your own commitment to growth by sharing what you're learning, admitting knowledge gaps, and seeking feedback.

To create a truly impactful learning culture, it's essential to move beyond ad hoc initiatives and build intentional, ongoing systems that support team growth. Bridging the gap between immediate delivery and structured development ensures that DevRel teams remain adaptable, motivated, and prepared for future challenges.

Creating Structured Learning Paths

Effective learning in DevRel requires more than just encouragement—it needs structure and direction:

- **Map critical competencies:** Identify the technical, communication, strategic, and leadership skills most important for your team's success.
- **Assess current capabilities:** Create honest assessments of where team members stand relative to needed competencies.
- **Develop personalized growth plans:** Work with each team member to create individualized learning road maps aligned with both organizational needs and personal interests.
- **Provide diverse learning resources:** Offer multiple learning formats (courses, peer mentoring, project assignments, shadowing) to accommodate different learning styles.

- **Build reflection rituals:** Establish regular check-ins focused specifically on learning progress and application.

Establishing structured learning paths is only part of the journey; the next step is to ensure that these systems foster meaningful growth and adaptability. To truly strengthen your DevRel team, it's vital to reflect on and learn from both successes and setbacks, transforming individual and collective experiences into ongoing improvement.

Learning From Successes and Failures

Some of the most valuable learning comes from thoughtfully examining our own experiences:

- **Implement retrospectives:** Conduct structured reviews after significant initiatives to extract lessons and identify improvement opportunities.
- **Create psychological safety:** Build an environment where team members feel safe discussing mistakes and challenges without fear of judgment.
- **Document and share learnings:** Capture insights from successes and failures in accessible formats that benefit the entire team.
- **Adapt approaches based on evidence:** Demonstrate how learning influences future decisions and approaches, creating a visible feedback loop.

By embedding these practices into your team's operations, you transform learning from an occasional activity into a continuous process that drives increasing effectiveness over time.

The Evolving Future of Developer Relations

The DevRel function continues to evolve rapidly as technology landscapes shift, developer needs change, and organizations recognize the strategic importance of developer experience. As a DevRel leader, anticipating and shaping this evolution is a critical part of your role.

Emerging Trends in DevRel Leadership

Several key trends are reshaping how effective DevRel leaders approach their work:

- **Deeper business integration:** DevRel is increasingly recognized as a strategic function rather than a marketing or engineering add-on, with corresponding expectations for business impact and measurement.
- **Expanded scope of influence:** Forward-thinking DevRel leaders are extending their impact beyond traditional developer audiences to influence product strategy, business models, and organizational priorities.
- **Data-driven decision-making:** Successful DevRel teams are developing sophisticated measurement frameworks that connect their activities to meaningful business and developer outcomes.
- **Experience orchestration:** Rather than owning discrete touchpoints, DevRel leaders are increasingly responsible for coordinating cohesive developer experiences across multiple functions and channels.
- **AI-enhanced operations:** Strategic leaders thoughtfully integrate AI tools to amplify team capabilities while maintaining the human expertise and authenticity that define effective DevRel.

As DevRel continues to adapt to new challenges and opportunities, staying proactive is essential. Bridging lessons learned with emerging trends ensures that your team remains both resilient and forward-thinking, ready to excel in an ever-changing environment.

Preparing Your Team for Future Success

As these trends reshape DevRel practice, strategic leaders must prepare their teams to thrive in this evolving landscape:

- **Develop strategic capabilities:** Build your team's ability to think systemically, connect to business objectives, and navigate organizational dynamics—skills that will only become more important.

- **Embrace intentional experimentation:** Create structured approaches to testing new ideas, evaluating outcomes, and scaling successful innovations.
- **Build adaptive systems:** Design programs and processes flexible enough to evolve as developer needs and organizational priorities shift.
- **Invest in cross-functional fluency:** Help your team develop the vocabulary, perspectives, and relationships to collaborate effectively across organizational boundaries.
- **Maintain technical credibility:** Even as strategic skills become more important, ensure your team maintains the technical depth that forms the foundation of authentic developer relationships.

By anticipating these shifts and intentionally developing the capabilities to address them, you position your team to remain effective and relevant as the DevRel function continues to evolve.

PERSONAL LEADERSHIP DEVELOPMENT PLAN

The following exercise is designed to help you take an intentional approach to your own leadership growth. By reflecting on your strengths, setting clear goals, and mapping actionable steps, you'll create a personalized road map for advancing your strategic capabilities as a DevRel leader.

1. Conduct a self-assessment by rating your comfort level (1–5) with strategic leadership areas: business strategy alignment, cross-functional communication, data-driven decision-making, executive presence, and change management.
2. Identify three key leadership capabilities you want to develop in the next 6 months. Define what success looks like and establish concrete metrics for tracking progress. For example, if your goal is to improve presenting to executives, you could define success in terms of increased confidence, positive executive feedback, fewer follow-up questions, and more frequent opportunities to present to senior leadership.

3. Develop a detailed action plan for each goal that outlines specific actions, required resources, an implementation timeline, and strategies for overcoming potential obstacles.
4. Identify potential mentors, cross-functional partners, external community members, and industry peers who can support your leadership development.
5. Establish monthly check-ins with an accountability partner to track progress, adjust strategies based on feedback, celebrate achievements, and refine goals as needed. This could be your manager, cross-functional collaborators, or your reporting team.

To systematize your leadership development plan, schedule a recurring monthly review to update your progress, adjust goals as needed, and document insights. Consider using a shared template or digital tool to track actions and outcomes, making it easy to revisit and refine your plan regularly.

Conclusion: From Tactical to Strategic DevRel

The transformation from tactical to strategic DevRel doesn't happen overnight. It requires intentional shifts in thinking, processes, and organizational relationships. However, this evolution is essential for DevRel functions to deliver their full potential value to developers and the business.

Strategic DevRel doesn't abandon tactical excellence. Instead, it elevates those activities by connecting them to clear strategic outcomes, measuring their impact on business and developer success, and positioning them within a coherent program framework.

As you continue your leadership journey, remember that strategic leadership isn't just about what you do—it's about enabling your team to achieve more than they could individually. By creating clear direction, building supportive systems, and fostering continuous learning, you multiply your impact far beyond what you could accomplish through personal execution alone.

CHAPTER 10

Aligning with Business Outcomes

Metrics transform abstract Developer Relations goals into concrete targets and create a shared language across the organization. For DevRel teams, metrics prove value and act as essential tools for maximizing impact.

DevRel teams that connect their activities to organizational objectives survive and thrive through organizational changes and budget cycles. Those without this visible alignment often find themselves vulnerable when resources become constrained, regardless of their impact.

This chapter presents practical approaches to DevRel measurement that create clarity without oversimplification. We'll focus on turning measurement into a strategic advantage that enhances your team's impact rather than merely documenting it.

The Strategic Necessity of Measurement

Without visible business alignment, DevRel teams face an uncomfortable reality—they become vulnerable during organizational changes and budget reviews. It doesn't matter how much value you create if stakeholders can't see and understand it in terms that matter to them.

Why Metrics Create Organizational Currency

Metrics do more than prove value. They create a shared language that transcends departmental boundaries. When you can demonstrate how your work connects to metrics that Sales, Marketing, Product, and Engineering already care about, something powerful happens—you transform from a cost center into a strategic partner.

K. Kemple, *Effective DevRel*, https://doi.org/10.1007/979-8-8688-2373-2_10

The most effective DevRel teams don't just measure their activities. They deliberately connect their work to existing organizational frameworks and speak the language that different stakeholders already understand:

- If Sales tracks customer acquisition cost (CAC), show how developer education programs reduce sales cycle length.
- If Product focuses on feature adoption rates, illustrate how DevRel-led tutorials and documentation improvements boost usage.
- If Marketing measures engagement rates, highlight how developer community initiatives increase time spent on company platforms.

By speaking the language of metrics that other departments already value, you elevate the perceived importance of DevRel within the organization. This isn't about manipulation—it's about creating clear connections between developer success and business outcomes that everyone can understand and rally behind.

The Vulnerability of Unmeasured Impact

Teams that struggle to articulate their impact beyond vague references to "awareness" or "developer engagement" face disproportionate scrutiny during resource constraints. The symptoms are clear:

- **Difficulty explaining impact:** Team members struggle to articulate how their work contributes to company success.
- **Reactive calendar:** The team's road map consists primarily of responding to requests rather than driving strategic initiatives.
- **Measurement gaps:** Success metrics focus on activities (content produced, events attended) rather than outcomes.
- **Budget vulnerability:** DevRel faces scrutiny because its connection to business outcomes isn't clearly established.

Effective measurement transforms DevRel from a perceived cost into a strategic investment with clear, demonstrable returns.

Leading vs. Lagging Indicators

One of the fundamental challenges in DevRel measurement is understanding the relationship between touchpoints and convergence points in the developer journey. As defined in Chapter 3, touchpoints are discrete interactions between developers and your company, while convergence points are critical milestones where multiple touchpoints culminate in significant shifts in the developer relationship.

This relationship provides a natural framework for understanding leading and lagging indicators in DevRel measurement. Effective measurement requires balancing both types in a connected framework.

Leading Indicators: Measuring Touchpoints

Leading indicators measure the touchpoints throughout the developer journey. These metrics share several characteristics:

- **Interaction-focused:** They measure specific moments of engagement.
- **High frequency:** They generate numerous data points across the journey.
- **Directly influenceable:** Your team can control these interactions.
- **Predictive potential:** Patterns of engagement indicate likely progression toward convergence points.

Examples include content engagement, documentation usage, sample code downloads, community interactions, and initial setup activities. While these metrics don't directly represent business value, they provide essential signals about developers' progression toward meaningful outcomes.

Lagging Indicators: Measuring Milestones

Lagging indicators measure the convergence points where multiple interactions culminate in significant shifts in the developer's relationship with your product. These metrics typically

- **Represent relationship milestones:** They mark meaningful changes in developer adoption.
- **Connect to business outcomes:** They relate directly to organizational objectives.
- **Result from multiple touchpoints:** They emerge from several preceding interactions.
- **Indicate relationship progression:** They signal substantive advances in platform adoption.

Examples include successful application or resource creation, production implementation or deployments, ecosystem integration, feature expansion, and positive Net Promoter Score (NPS) ratings. These metrics matter most to the organization because they represent substantive progress in the developer relationship.

Defining Meaningful Lagging Indicators

The struggle most DevRel teams face isn't tracking activities—it's defining what actually constitutes success. Slack's platform team defines an activated developer as someone who creates an app or workflow with 3+ user-days in a 7-day period within 30 days of first interaction. Stripe considers a developer activated once they've processed their first live transaction. Twilio tracks developers who've sent 100+ messages in production within the first month. The specific thresholds matter less than having clear, measurable definitions that connect to business outcomes. These concrete metrics let you move beyond vague claims about "developer engagement" and instead say "42% of developers who complete our tutorial activate within 14 days, compared to 18% who skip it"—the kind of statement that makes product and sales teams pay attention.

How Leading and Lagging Indicators Connect

The most effective measurement approach shows how touchpoints lead to convergence points in coherent chains:

> Touchpoints (Leading) ➤ Engagement Patterns ➤ Convergence Points (Lagging) ➤ Business Impact

Consider this example for a content program focused on improving developer activation:

1. **Touchpoints:** Tutorial views, documentation views, workshop attendance, CLI usage
2. **Engagement patterns:** Completion of educational sequence, progressive code implementation
3. **Convergence point:** Successful first application deployment
4. **Business impact:** Transition from exploration to active implementation

This connected approach helps you identify which touchpoint patterns drive developers toward important convergence points, allowing you to optimize resources toward the interactions that most effectively guide developers to success.

Using Metrics for Strategic Alignment

Understanding leading and lagging indicators provides the foundation for measurement. But creating organizational impact requires deliberately using these metrics to build alignment across teams and demonstrate strategic value.

Building Cross-Functional Alignment

One of the most powerful aspects of a well-designed metrics approach is its ability to foster cross-functional alignment. Rather than creating separate metrics for each team, effective measurement includes work done across marketing, developer relations, and developer experience teams, regardless of who is responsible for specific tactics.

This approach creates several strategic advantages:

- **Unified goals:** Shared metrics create a common language and objectives for teams that might otherwise operate in silos.
- **Holistic representation:** Whether a marketing campaign drives new usage, a DevRel initiative improves documentation, or a Developer Experience team adds a new feature, these metrics capture the impact of each team's efforts.

- **Collaborative improvement:** When metrics change, it prompts cross-team discussions about root causes and opportunities.
- **Balanced attribution:** This methodology promotes shared accountability, discouraging individual teams from claiming exclusive success or shouldering complete responsibility for challenges.
- **Strategic alignment:** Shared metrics make it easier to align strategies across teams during planning sessions and feedback reviews.

By implementing shared metrics, you're not just measuring platform growth—you're fostering a culture of shared responsibility for developer success. This approach recognizes the interconnected nature of work across teams and celebrates collective impact on the developer journey.

Implementing Alignment Mechanisms

Creating shared metrics is only the first step. To truly align DevRel with other departments, you need deliberate mechanisms that embed collaboration into your operating rhythm:

- **Regular cross-team syncs:** Establish recurring meetings where DevRel, Product, Marketing, and Engineering teams share updates and align on priorities.
- **Shared OKRs and North Star Metrics:** Work with other teams to create Objectives and Key Results that span departments and encourage collaboration. Identify a North Star Metric that all teams can rally behind.
- **Unified data dashboards:** Develop dashboards that showcase how DevRel efforts impact metrics across different teams, similar to how Growth teams maintain company-wide growth dashboards.
- **Collaborative content strategy:** Partner with Marketing and Product teams to create a content calendar that serves multiple purposes, from developer education to product promotion.
- **Shared planning sessions:** Include DevRel in product road map planning sessions and marketing campaign brainstorms to ensure the developer perspective is considered from the outset.

Growth teams are masters of cross-functional collaboration, and DevRel can learn from their playbook. Companies like Spotify organize cross-functional "squads," Airbnb holds weekly experiment review meetings with all relevant teams, and LinkedIn uses shared OKRs to ensure alignment across product teams. DevRel can adopt similar approaches to create strong cross-functional partnerships.

Communicating Your Measurement Strategy

Beyond demonstrating business value, effective DevRel leaders develop communication approaches tailored to different stakeholders and situations. Your ability to influence without direct authority depends heavily on how well you can present your measurement strategy.

Executive Leadership Communication

Aligning DevRel leadership is essential for maximizing impact and driving consistent prioritization across the organization. By intentionally connecting metrics, strategies, and communication practices to clear executive communication, DevRel can build stronger leadership support and create top-down momentum for business objectives.

When communicating with executive leadership about your metrics

- Focus on business outcomes first, activities second
- Present information in concise, visually oriented formats
- Connect DevRel initiatives to strategic company priorities
- Use stories that illustrate key points with concrete examples
- Anticipate and address potential concerns proactively
- Offer clear next steps and decision points when needed

Building executive relationships requires more than periodic presentations. It means cultivating connections based on delivering value and addressing their priorities. Use quantitative and qualitative evidence to create compelling cases for developer experience investments. Implement systems that make developer success and challenges visible throughout the organization.

Cross-Functional Leadership Communication

DevRel's success depends almost entirely on your ability to work effectively across functions—with product, engineering, marketing, sales, and more. But here's the challenge: each team has its own goals, metrics, and constraints, and you're often asking for their time and resources. The way you frame your collaboration makes the difference between being seen as a strategic partner vs. another competing priority.

When working with peers across functions

- Emphasize shared goals and mutual benefits
- Acknowledge constraints and competing priorities
- Propose collaborative approaches rather than competing demands
- Demonstrate an understanding of their functional priorities

The language you use significantly impacts how your intentions are perceived. Instead of saying "we should own this," try "how can we contribute to this?" Instead of "this isn't working," frame it as "what outcomes are we trying to achieve?" Language that focuses on contribution rather than criticism builds receptivity to your ideas.

Creating Your Strategic Positioning

With a clear measurement framework and alignment mechanisms in place, you can define DevRel's unique position within your organization. Effective positioning requires more than a statement—you need a compelling narrative.

Your narrative should explain

- **Why these metrics matter:** The impact on developers and business outcomes
- **Why DevRel is uniquely suited:** The specific capabilities that make DevRel the right function to drive these outcomes
- **How success will be measured:** Clear metrics and milestones that demonstrate impact
- **What resources are required:** Realistic assessment of what's needed to succeed

This narrative helps stakeholders understand the strategic value of your positioning and builds support for your approach. Without it, you're just another team asking for budget and headcount.

Strategic program development works future-back instead of present-forward. Define the desired future state you want to achieve in 12–18 months, identify key enabling conditions that must happen for those outcomes to occur, map critical DevRel capabilities essential to create those conditions, design coherent programs that will build and apply those capabilities, and establish progress indicators to measure movement toward the desired future state.

Using Metrics to Drive Resource Allocation

Perhaps the most powerful application of a strong measurement framework is its ability to influence resource allocation decisions. When you can demonstrate clear connections between DevRel activities and business outcomes, you transform budget conversations from cost justification to investment optimization.

Effective resource allocation requires

- **Data-driven narratives:** Use quantitative and qualitative evidence to create compelling cases for investments.
- **Clear ROI demonstration:** Show how previous investments generated measurable returns.
- **Strategic prioritization:** Demonstrate how requested resources align with company priorities.
- **Risk mitigation:** Articulate the business risks of not making the investment.

This strategic influence enables DevRel leaders to shape decisions and priorities far beyond their direct scope of control. It transforms DevRel from a function that responds to organizational decisions into one that actively shapes them.

Defining Success Metrics

To implement an effective metrics framework based on the relationship between touchpoints and convergence points, identify the four to six most crucial convergence points in your developer journey. For each, define

1. **Clear milestone definition:** Establish clear criteria for success for this convergence point. For example, "first application deployed" might require specific feature usage to be meaningful.
2. **Lagging indicator:** Define the metric that confirms this convergence point has been reached. It should be an observable, measurable event that conclusively demonstrates the achievement of the milestone.
3. **Business alignment:** Identify which business metrics are most directly influenced by this convergence point. This creates a direct connection between developer progress and organizational objectives.
4. **Leading indicator patterns:** Map which combinations of touchpoints most reliably predict achievement of this convergence point. This helps you identify which early activities deserve the most attention and optimization.
5. **Measurement timeframes:** Establish reasonable expectations for when convergence point metrics should materialize after relevant touchpoint activities. This prevents premature judgment of initiative effectiveness.

This focused approach ensures you're measuring what matters most for both developer success and business impact rather than tracking every possible metric. Concentrating on the critical convergence points creates a manageable measurement framework that connects daily activities to strategic outcomes.

CREATING YOUR DEVREL DASHBOARD

Let's put these measurement concepts into practice by building a practical DevRel dashboard. Follow these steps to create a measurement framework that connects your activities to business impact:

1. **Reference your convergence points:** Identify four to six key milestones in your developer journey that represent significant shifts in the relationship (e.g., first deployment, production usage).
2. **Connect touchpoints:** List the leading indicators (touchpoints) that typically precede each convergence point. Focus on measurable interactions that you can track.
3. **Define indicator relationships:** For each touchpoint, identify its corresponding leading indicators that measure early engagement, and for each convergence point, determine the lagging indicators that confirm achievement of significant milestones.
4. **Establish measurement cadence:** Determine how frequently you'll measure each metric and what timeframes are appropriate for showing progress.
5. **Create visualization:** Build a dashboard that shows the relationship between your touchpoints and convergence points. This will make it easy to track progress and identify patterns.

When building your dashboard, remember to

- Focus on metrics that directly connect to business objectives
- Include both leading and lagging indicators
- Make the relationships between metrics clear and visible
- Keep it simple enough to be actionable

Review and refine your dashboard quarterly to ensure it continues to provide meaningful insights about the effectiveness of your DevRel program.

Conclusion: Metrics as Organizational Currency

Effective metrics transform DevRel from perception-based activities to data-informed strategy. This chapter distinguished between leading and lagging indicators, showing how they connect to demonstrate real business impact. By identifying your most crucial convergence points and building measurement frameworks around them, DevRel teams can focus resources on interactions that genuinely matter while creating clear connections between daily work and strategic outcomes.

But measurement alone doesn't create impact. The real power comes from using metrics as organizational currency—a shared language that enables cross-functional collaboration, builds executive support, and drives resource allocation decisions. When you can speak the language of metrics that Sales, Marketing, Product, and Engineering already value, you transform DevRel from a cost center into a strategic investment.

This strategic use of measurement elevates DevRel's importance within the organization. It enables you to influence decisions far beyond your direct scope of control, shape priorities across departments, and build the business cases needed to secure resources for high-impact initiatives. Most importantly, it protects your team from the vulnerability that comes with unmeasured impact.

The measurement framework you build today becomes the foundation for all subsequent strategic work. It enables you to move from random acts of DevRel to coherent programs with clear outcomes. It transforms budget conversations from cost justification to investment optimization. And it positions DevRel as an essential strategic partner rather than a nice-to-have function.

Remember, effective measurement isn't about tracking every possible metric. It's about creating clarity on what matters most and connecting your daily activities to outcomes that resonate across the entire organization.

CHAPTER 11

Moving from Random Acts to Programs

Even the most strategically designed DevRel function faces fundamental challenges: how to scale impact without proportionally scaling the team and how to allocate limited resources effectively. This chapter combines operational systems that amplify impact with prioritization frameworks that ensure your team focuses on what matters most.

We'll explore how to break the "Yet Another Program" cycle that traps growing DevRel teams, implement practical prioritization through the Drop-Defer-Delegate framework, balance execution with communication, and identify high-value automation opportunities. These aren't theoretical exercises—they're practical systems for building a DevRel function that delivers consistent impact without burning out your team.

Countering "Yet Another Program" Syndrome

The cross-functional nature of Developer Relations creates a unique challenge called "Yet Another Program" (YAP). DevRel professionals typically need to reach further, both internally and externally, than those in adjacent teams, creating two significant pressure points:

1. Higher skill requirements: The role demands a broader range of cross-functional competencies.
2. Increased alignment needs: The further the work extends beyond the immediate team, the more alignment is required.

As DevRel teams take on more initiatives, program management overhead grows exponentially—often leading to decreased output rather than increased impact.

K. Kemple, *Effective DevRel*, https://doi.org/10.1007/979-8-8688-2373-2_11

Understanding the YAP Cycle

YAP follows a predictable pattern:

1. **Opportunity identification:** The team spots a new way to serve developers.
2. **Program creation:** A new initiative launches to address the opportunity.
3. **Initial success:** The program shows promising early results.
4. **Expansion pressure:** Stakeholders request similar programs for other areas.
5. **Operational strain:** The team struggles to maintain quality across growing programs.
6. **Execution inconsistency:** Programs receive uneven attention based on immediate demands.
7. **Impact dilution:** Overall effectiveness decreases despite increased activity.

Recognizing these recurring patterns is the first step toward meaningful change. To truly overcome the pitfalls of YAP, DevRel teams must rethink not just what they do, but how they operate—shifting focus from reactive program launches to building resilient, scalable foundations.

Breaking the YAP Cycle

Breaking this cycle requires shifting from an opportunity-driven approach to an operations-first mindset. The goal isn't to do fewer things—it's to create systems that allow you to do more things with greater consistency and lower overhead.

This transformation requires moving from traditional program management to program architecture. In traditional program management, each program has custom processes where success depends on the specific program manager's approaches. Knowledge lives primarily with key individuals, and scaling requires proportional team growth.

Program architecture takes a different approach. Programs follow standardized templates and frameworks where success depends on well-designed systems and processes. Knowledge is embedded in documentation and workflows, and scaling happens through system optimization, not just team growth.

Building scalable program foundations requires investing in three core operational elements:

1. **Repeatable:** Creating consistent processes that maintain quality.
2. **Teachable:** Developing well-documented workflows that anyone can learn.
3. **Measurable:** Implementing clear metrics that demonstrate impact.

By adopting an operations-first mindset and investing in foundational program architecture, DevRel teams position themselves to scale impact sustainably. This shift not only streamlines processes but also empowers teams to pursue strategic growth without sacrificing quality or overextending resources.

Note At Slack, we transformed our customer enablement program by separating program management from technical participation. Our DevRel Manager took ownership of program strategy, logistics coordination, stakeholder relationships, and cross-program measurement. Developer Advocates focused on content creation, workshop delivery, technical insights, and developer relationships. This approach ensured everyone was doing work directly related to their actual responsibilities and competencies. It was a clear demonstration of how operational systems can dramatically expand what a team achieves without adding headcount or burning out existing team members.

Drop, Defer, Delegate: A Practical Prioritization Framework

When faced with more opportunities than capacity, many DevRel teams attempt everything—working longer hours, sacrificing quality, or burning out team members. The Drop, Defer, Delegate framework provides a structured alternative for making intentional decisions about where to invest limited resources.

Drop: The Courage to Say No

Dropping activities requires acknowledging that not everything represents the best use of your limited resources, even if those activities have intrinsic value. The key is distinguishing between activities that feel productive and those that genuinely advance strategic priorities.

Candidates for dropping include

1. **Low-alignment activities:** Initiatives that don't directly support your strategic priorities.
2. **Limited-impact efforts:** Work where the potential benefit doesn't justify the required investment.
3. **Diminishing return programs:** Established activities whose effectiveness has declined.
4. **Not-your-job responsibilities:** Functions that are better owned by other teams.
5. **Outdated traditions:** Activities maintained primarily because "we've always done them."

Making the decision to drop activities becomes easier when you can point to the higher value work you'll pursue instead.

Defer: Strategic Timing of Initiatives

Deferring recognizes that many initiatives have genuine value but not necessarily at the present moment. Strategic deferral creates space for current priorities while preserving future opportunities.

Candidates for deferring include

- **Promising but premature initiatives:** Ideas with potential that depend on not-yet-established foundations.
- **Sequencing-dependent programs:** Activities that would be more effective after other work completes.
- **Resource-constrained opportunities:** Initiatives that require capabilities or bandwidth are not currently available.

- **Future-aligned priorities:** Programs that will have greater relevance in upcoming product or business cycles.
- **Good-but-not-urgent ideas:** Valuable concepts that don't address immediate strategic needs.

The discipline of deferral prevents good ideas from becoming distractions while ensuring they remain available when circumstances change.

Delegate: Expanding Your Impact Through Others

Delegation recognizes that impact isn't limited to your direct work but includes what you enable others to accomplish. Effective delegation multiplies your team's capacity while developing capabilities across the organization.

Delegation opportunities include

- **Appropriate cross-functional work:** Activities better aligned with other teams' core responsibilities.
- **Growth-enabling responsibilities:** Tasks that provide development opportunities for team members.
- **Community contribution opportunities:** Work that engaged community members could effectively handle.
- **Specialized execution:** Functions requiring expertise your team doesn't need to maintain internally.
- **Operational tasks:** Routine activities that support resources could handle.

Implementing effective delegation starts with matching tasks to capabilities—ensuring the delegate has or can develop necessary skills. Define clear expectations by establishing specific outcomes, success criteria, and completion timelines. Provide necessary support through resources, context, and access to information. Create feedback mechanisms for regular check-ins and course correction. Recognize contributions by acknowledging the delegate's work and impact.

Effective delegation requires more upfront investment than doing work yourself, but it creates sustainable capacity expansion and develops organizational capability beyond your immediate team.

Communicating Resource Allocation Decisions

Resource allocation decisions become significantly easier when you establish clear communication patterns with stakeholders. Transparency about constraints and criteria builds trust and reduces conflict around priority decisions.

Share your team's capacity limitations transparently. Explain the criteria and processes used for allocation. Establish clear channels for stakeholders to submit resource requests. Publish planning cycles and decision points, and define emergency protocols for unexpected high-priority needs.

Delivering Constructive "No" Messages

When unable to accommodate requests, deliver responses that maintain relationships and preserve future collaboration opportunities:

- Acknowledge the value of the request from the stakeholder's perspective.
- Explain the broader prioritization landscape and competing demands.
- Offer alternative approaches or reduced-scope options when appropriate.
- Indicate when reconsideration might be possible.
- Thank stakeholders for their understanding and collaboration.

These elements transform rejections into collaborative conversations about priorities and possibilities.

Building Stakeholder Partnerships

Move beyond transactional request fulfillment to collaborative planning. Establish regular touchpoints independent of specific requests. Create shared road maps that integrate priorities. Give stakeholders visibility into emerging constraints. Help stakeholders understand DevRel priorities and develop joint metrics that transcend individual initiatives.

These partnership practices transform stakeholders from requestors into collaborators who understand your constraints and work with you to find mutually beneficial solutions.

The Execution-Communication Balance

Successful DevRel functions maintain a critical balance between doing the work and communicating about it. Many teams focus too heavily on one side, either concentrating solely on execution without sufficient communication or overemphasizing communication without adequate delivery.

The Communication-Execution Continuum

Consider this balance as a continuum with risks at either extreme. Understanding these risks helps teams find the productive middle ground.

Teams focusing almost exclusively on execution face several risks:

- Stakeholders lose visibility and forget the project's importance.
- Resource commitments become vulnerable during budget constraints.
- Work is perceived as less valuable without an impact context.
- Team contributions go unrecognized, affecting morale and influence.

Teams emphasizing communication over execution face different risks:

- Excessive updates create "all talk, no action" perception.
- Time spent on communication reduces execution capacity.
- Premature sharing of partial work creates confusion.
- Stakeholders discount communication without seeing results.

The optimal approach occupies the middle ground—sufficient execution to deliver meaningful progress with appropriate communication to maintain visibility and support.

Strategies for Maintaining Balance

One of the biggest tensions in DevRel is the constant pull between doing the work and talking about the work. Stakeholders need visibility into what you're accomplishing, but if you spend all your time reporting on progress, you're not making any. The solution isn't choosing between execution and communication—it's building systems that make your work visible as you go.

Create execution visibility through

- Public road maps showing planned work and progress
- Regular demo sessions to show rather than tell
- Progress dashboards tracking key metrics
- Release notes documenting completed work and value
- User stories showing impact on developers

These mechanisms provide stakeholders with visibility while minimizing the time your team spends on status updates. The key is creating systems that communicate progress as a byproduct of your work rather than as separate communication activities.

Intentional Automation of Routine Tasks

Automation represents one of the most powerful operational levers for DevRel teams. By thoughtfully automating routine tasks, you free team capacity for high-value work while often improving consistency and reliability.

Identifying Automation Opportunities

Focus automation efforts on three categories of work. Each category offers distinct benefits and requires different implementation approaches.

High-frequency, low-variability tasks represent the clearest automation candidates. These activities occur regularly with predictable patterns, making them ideal for standardization. Examples include resource distribution and updates, status reporting and metrics collection, basic community management functions, content publishing workflows, and event registration and management.

Error-prone manual processes benefit particularly from automation because reducing human error can significantly improve reliability. Focus on automating cross-platform consistency verification, documentation version synchronization, regression testing for code examples, communication coordination across channels, and data aggregation from multiple sources.

Coordination-intensive activities often involve multiple handoffs and approval steps that create delays and confusion. Automation can streamline multistep approval workflows, cross-team collaboration processes, external partner synchronization, community contribution management, and complex event logistics.

Balanced Automation Approaches

Effective DevRel automation balances efficiency with human connection through augmentation vs. replacement. Use automation to handle routine elements while preserving human involvement for high-value interactions. Implement "human-in-the-loop" workflows where automation handles preparation and processing while humans make key decisions. Create systems that reduce administrative overhead without removing genuine human connection.

Progressive automation implementation starts with simple, bounded processes with precise inputs and outputs. Validate results thoroughly before expanding automation scope. Monitor for unintended consequences, especially regarding community experience, and increase sophistication gradually based on demonstrated success.

OPERATIONAL ASSESSMENT

Operational excellence sounds great in theory, but in practice, most DevRel teams are too buried in day-to-day work to step back and evaluate how they're actually operating. The irony is that this lack of reflection often perpetuates the very inefficiencies of keeping you overwhelmed. This exercise is designed to give you that necessary perspective—not as busy work, but as a strategic investment that will reveal where small changes can create outsized improvements in your team's effectiveness.

Apply these steps to evaluate and improve your DevRel operations:

1. Audit current operational processes:
    a. List all recurring tasks and activities.
    b. Document current automation and workflows.

c. Identify manual bottlenecks and pain points.

d. Note areas where work frequently gets delayed.

2. Map resource allocation patterns:

    a. Review how time is currently distributed across initiatives.

    b. Document which stakeholders receive what portion of resources.

    c. Identify areas where resources feel consistently strained.

    d. Note any patterns in emergency resource requests.

3. Evaluate communication effectiveness:

    a. Review current communication channels and cadence.

    b. Document feedback received about visibility and updates.

    c. Assess stakeholder understanding of your work.

    d. Note areas where communication gaps create friction.

4. Analyze automation opportunities:

    a. List tasks that occur at least weekly.

    b. Identify processes that frequently have errors.

    c. Document coordination-heavy workflows.

    d. Note areas where manual effort creates delays.

5. Create an improvement action plan:

    a. Prioritize top operational pain points.

    b. Define specific improvement initiatives.

    c. Set measurable success criteria.

    d. Create a timeline for implementing changes.

This assessment will likely surface more opportunities than you can tackle immediately. Take your findings and prioritize by impact vs. effort—start with quick wins that remove significant friction, then move to higher-effort improvements addressing critical bottlenecks. Schedule a quarterly review to repeat this audit, as operational drift happens fast. Share your improvement plan with stakeholders so they understand why certain operational investments matter for long-term effectiveness.

Conclusion: From Execution to Operation

The tension between doing great work and having the capacity to do great work is one of DevRel's defining challenges. Without operational systems, growth creates more problems than it solves—more programs mean more coordination, more stakeholders mean more alignment meetings, and more success paradoxically leads to less effectiveness.

What makes operational excellence particularly important for DevRel is that our value lies in the quality of our engagement and the depth of our insights, not just the volume of our output. Systems that reduce coordination overhead don't just save time—they preserve the mental space needed for the kind of thoughtful work that actually serves developers well.

The frameworks in this chapter—countering YAP syndrome, strategic prioritization, execution visibility, and thoughtful automation—all address the same fundamental truth: sustainable impact requires building systems that work for you rather than managing an ever-growing collection of programs that work against you.

Your operational maturity directly determines how much strategic work your team can actually accomplish. Teams drowning in program management overhead can't identify emerging developer needs, spot competitive threats, or shape product direction—even when they have the talent and insight to do so. Operational excellence isn't about efficiency for its own sake. It's about creating the conditions where your team's expertise can actually make a difference.

CHAPTER 12

Building Sustainable Teams

Building an effective Developer Relations team requires intentional design that guides and maximizes organic growth. The most successful DevRel teams have clear structures aligned with business goals, thoughtful hiring practices, strategic work distribution, and systems that prevent dependency on specific individuals. This chapter explores how to build and scale teams that deliver consistent value while avoiding common pitfalls.

Creating Intentional Team Structures

Your team structure should reflect your specific organizational context and priorities. The structure you choose isn't just an organizational chart exercise—it directly impacts your team's ability to deliver value to developers and your business.

Understanding your organizational context is the first step in designing an effective DevRel team. Different environments require different approaches, influencing everything from team size and composition to reporting relationships and operational focus.

Organizational Context

The shape and structure of your DevRel team must be thoughtfully designed to fit your organization's specific context. As explored in Chapter 2 (Navigating Organizational Context), different organizational environments create significantly different requirements for DevRel teams. Before designing your team structure, consider how these key contextual factors will influence your approach.

K. Kemple, *Effective DevRel*, https://doi.org/10.1007/979-8-8688-2373-2_12

Company Stage

Your company's growth stage fundamentally shapes your DevRel team structure and capabilities. A three-person startup has vastly different needs than an enterprise with thousands of customers, and your team design must reflect these realities. The maturity of your organization determines not just team size but also the level of specialization you can support and the processes you need to implement.

- **Startup:** Small teams (one to three people) typically require generalists who can cover multiple functions with a flat structure.
- **Scale-up:** Growing organizations benefit from specialized roles (content, community, advocacy) with a dedicated DevRel leader.
- **Enterprise:** Mature organizations may need complex structures with multiple specialized teams, regional focuses, and product-specific advocacy. It's worth noting that not all enterprises will have sizable DevRel teams, and you might be required to wear multiple hats, like in smaller companies.

As your company grows, your DevRel structure should evolve to match increasing complexity while maintaining the agility that makes DevRel effective. The key is recognizing when specialization creates value vs. when it creates unnecessary coordination overhead.

Business Model

How developers fit into your buying process profoundly influences your DevRel approach. Companies where developers control purchasing decisions need different structures than those where developers influence but don't control the budget. Understanding this distinction helps you build teams that address the right audiences with the right messages. The two business models can be categorized as

1. Developer-first companies (where developers are both users and buyers) typically emphasize technical depth with close alignment to product teams.
2. Developer+ companies (where developers are users, but others influence purchasing) often need structures that bridge technical and business contexts.

This business model distinction affects everything from the technical depth you need on your team to how you measure success. In developer-first companies, you'll spend more time translating technical and business value internally to stakeholders who may not be technical themselves. In developer+ companies, that translation work extends externally to bridge technical users with business decision-makers.

Organizational Placement

Where DevRel sits in your organizational chart shapes priorities, resources, and day-to-day focus. Each placement comes with natural advantages and constraints that influence how you structure your team and define success. Understanding these dynamics helps you work with rather than against your organizational reality:

- DevRel in Marketing typically emphasizes content production and campaign alignment.
- DevRel in Product/Engineering often focuses on technical advocacy and feedback collection.
- Standalone DevRel requires broader structures spanning awareness through adoption.

Your organizational placement isn't just about reporting lines—it fundamentally influences your team's priorities, the resources available to you, and how stakeholders perceive your work. Build your team structure to maximize the advantages of your placement while compensating for its natural limitations.

Common Structural Models

Most DevRel organizations adopt one of several structural models, each optimized for different contexts and challenges. These models aren't mutually exclusive—the most effective DevRel teams often combine elements of multiple approaches based on their specific needs. Understanding these models helps you make intentional choices about how to organize your team rather than defaulting to whatever structure feels familiar.

The right structure depends on your platform's complexity, your developer audience's diversity, and your organizational context. A simple platform serving a single developer persona might thrive with a function-aligned structure, while a complex platform serving multiple segments across regions might need a hybrid approach combining product, persona, and geographic elements.

- **Product-aligned:** Team members focus on specific products within your platform. This approach is effective when products have distinct technical characteristics or different developer audiences.
- **Function-aligned:** Teams organize around DevRel disciplines (advocacy, content, community). This approach works well when your platform presents a unified experience, and specialized expertise creates significant value.
- **Persona-aligned:** Teams organize around specific developer personas or segments (e.g., enterprise architects, front-end developers, data scientists). It is effective when your platform serves multiple technical communities with distinct needs that require specialized knowledge.
- **Journey-Aligned:** Teams organize around stages of the developer journey (discovery, activation, adoption). This approach is effective for complex, multistage developer experiences.
- **Geographic:** Regional structures layer on top of other models. It is important when developer communities have significant regional differences.

Most effective DevRel organizations implement hybrid structures combining elements of multiple models based on their specific needs and constraints. The key is choosing structures that align with your strategic priorities while remaining simple enough for your team to execute effectively.

Process Foundations

Beyond structure, effective teams need well-designed processes for content development, review, and publication; feedback collection, prioritization, and routing; event selection and execution; and cross-functional collaboration. The appropriate level of process formality depends on both team size and organizational context. Small teams in small companies typically need minimal formal processes, while small teams in larger organizations often require more comprehensive documentation and workflows to manage cross-functional collaboration at scale.

Hiring for DevRel Roles

Hiring the right people is critical in building an effective DevRel team. Unlike more established functions with standardized role definitions, DevRel positions often blend technical expertise, communication skills, and community engagement in unique combinations. This creates both challenges and opportunities in the hiring process.

Simply looking for people with "DevRel experience" isn't sufficient. Organizations have implemented DevRel so differently that someone successful in one context might struggle in another. Additionally, exceptional candidates might come from adjacent backgrounds—engineering, technical writing, product management, or community management—without formal DevRel titles.

Effective hiring starts with clearly defined responsibilities and competencies for each role, mapped to your organizational context and DevRel approach.

Core Competency Areas

DevRel roles require a unique blend of skills that rarely appear together in traditional job descriptions. Rather than looking for perfect candidates who excel at everything, identify which competencies matter most for your specific context and hire people with the right foundation who can grow into the role. The following competency areas represent the full spectrum of DevRel capabilities, but no single role requires mastery of all of them.

Technical Competencies

Technical credibility forms the foundation of effective DevRel work. Developers can immediately tell when someone understands their domain vs. when they're reciting talking points. The depth of technical knowledge you need varies by role and context—a Developer Advocate might need to write production-quality code, while a Technical Community Manager might need broader but shallower technical understanding across multiple domains.

The specific balance of technical competencies varies by role. Developer Advocates typically need more technical depth and hands-on coding ability, while Technical Writers require exceptional ability to understand and explain complex systems even if they don't build them themselves.

Communication Competencies

DevRel professionals must communicate effectively across wildly different contexts—from writing technical documentation to presenting at conferences to having one-on-one conversations with developers to explaining technical concepts to business stakeholders. Each of these requires different communication skills, and few people excel at all of them naturally.

Look for candidates who demonstrate strong communication skills in at least one or two of these areas, with the potential to develop others. Someone who writes exceptionally clear documentation can probably learn to present effectively with practice and coaching.

Strategic Competencies

Strategic thinking separates good DevRel practitioners from great ones. It's the difference between creating content because it seems like a good idea and creating content because you've identified a specific gap in the developer journey that's limiting adoption. These competencies often develop with experience, but you can identify candidates with strategic potential by looking for people who naturally think about context, priorities, and impact.

Strategic competencies typically matter more for senior roles, but even junior team members benefit from developing these skills early. Look for candidates who ask thoughtful questions about why and how, not just what they'll be doing.

Interpersonal Competencies

DevRel work is fundamentally about relationships—with developers, with internal teams, and with the broader community. Technical and communication skills get you in the door, but interpersonal competencies determine your long-term effectiveness and impact. These are often the hardest skills to teach, so pay close attention to them during the hiring process.

Strong interpersonal competencies matter across all DevRel roles. A technically brilliant advocate who can't build genuine relationships will struggle to create lasting impact, while someone with exceptional interpersonal skills can overcome gaps in other areas through collaboration and continuous learning.

Onboarding for Success

The first few months in a DevRel role significantly impact long-term effectiveness and retention. Unlike more established functions with standardized onboarding, DevRel roles often require customized approaches due to their cross-functional nature and varied responsibilities. A thoughtfully designed onboarding program accelerates time-to-first-contribution while building the foundation for sustained success.

Effective onboarding goes beyond basic orientation, addressing three critical dimensions that new team members need to master. Each dimension builds on the others—you can't provide meaningful organizational context without a technical foundation, and role clarification only makes sense once someone understands both the technology and the organization. Structure your onboarding to develop these dimensions progressively rather than trying to cover everything at once.

Technical Foundation

New team members need deep, hands-on familiarity with your platform before they can effectively advocate for it or create meaningful content. This goes beyond product training—it requires time to experiment, break things, and build a genuine understanding of how developers will actually use your technology. Provide comprehensive platform training, access to internal product and engineering resources, and sandbox environments for experimentation.

Organizational Context

DevRel's cross-functional nature means new team members must quickly understand how different parts of the organization work and where DevRel fits in the bigger picture. This context helps them navigate internal relationships, understand strategic priorities, and make better decisions about where to invest their time. Facilitate introductions to key stakeholders across functions, provide an overview of the business model and strategic priorities, and clearly explain how DevRel supports organizational goals.

Role Clarification

DevRel roles can feel ambiguous, especially to people coming from more structured functions. New team members need explicit discussion of responsibilities and expectations, introduction to relevant processes and workflows, and clear initial objectives and success metrics. This clarity reduces anxiety and helps people focus their energy productively.

A structured onboarding approach similar to the "90-Day Developer Relations Leadership Plan" (included in this book) can be adapted for all team members. This approach—focusing on Learn & Observe (first 30 days), Partner & Contribute (days 31–60), and Propose & Plan (days 61–90)—provides a clear progression from knowledge building to active contribution, with appropriate milestones for each phase. This structured progression builds confidence while ensuring that new team members develop sufficient context before making significant recommendations.

Distributing Work Effectively

One of the most challenging aspects of DevRel leadership is distributing work to maximize impact while preventing burnout. The unbounded nature of DevRel work means you'll always have more opportunities than capacity, making intentional work distribution essential for sustainable team performance.

Matching Work Complexity to Team Capabilities

Not all DevRel work requires the same level of expertise or experience. Understanding the different types of work and matching them appropriately to team members creates both efficiency and growth opportunities. When senior team members spend too much time on routine tasks, you waste their expertise and limit your team's capacity for complex initiatives. When junior team members get overwhelmed with work beyond their current capabilities, you create frustration and risk burnout.

Work varies in both complexity and volume, creating a natural distribution that looks like a pyramid. At the top, you have high-complexity, lower-volume work like program architecture, measurement frameworks, and strategic planning. This work typically requires extensive experience and systems thinking. In the middle, you have medium-complexity, medium-volume work like significant content creation, workshop development, and community program implementation. This work benefits from solid experience and specialized skills. At the bottom, you have lower-complexity, higher-volume work like routine community engagement, content updates, and event support. This work provides excellent learning opportunities for newer team members.

Effective distribution matches team members to appropriate work based on their experience, skills, and growth objectives. Teams commonly face challenges when there are too many senior members relative to high-complexity work, there aren't enough experienced members to handle complex initiatives, the team lacks mid-level contributors to bridge senior and junior members, or the team consists primarily of mid-level contributors with limited senior guidance. Address these imbalances through strategic hiring, professional development, partnerships with other functions, and thoughtful scope management.

Note I've been thinking about this for years—how vital the distribution of challenge is to a team's success. It's actually one of my primary considerations when managing. How many developers do you know who've left their job because either (1) the work is no longer challenging and there's no career growth, or (2) the work is too challenging and they have no support? Challenge plays an essential role in our happiness. I developed a model called the "Pyramid of Challenge" (see Appendix X) to think about this systematically.

Workload Management Systems

Beyond matching people to appropriate work types, implement systems to manage the overall workload. Without explicit systems, work distribution becomes reactive and often inequitable—with some team members chronically overloaded while others have spare capacity.

Create explicit models for team capacity that account for all work types, including preparation and "invisible" work, allocate time realistically across priorities, and reserve capacity for unexpected opportunities. The invisible work—prep time for talks, coordination with other teams, responding to developer questions—often consumes more time than the visible deliverables.

Develop frameworks for declining or deferring requests that align decisions with strategic priorities, provide constructive alternatives when possible, and explain rationales clearly and respectfully. Saying no thoughtfully is one of the most important skills in DevRel leadership.

Implement rotation systems for high-demand responsibilities, create primary/secondary ownership models for key areas, and ensure coverage during absences or transitions. These work distribution mechanisms prevent burnout from high-visibility responsibilities and create resilience when team members are unavailable.

These systems create sustainable work distribution that prevents overload and inefficient resource allocation.

Avoiding Single Points of Failure

In traditional architecture, a keystone is the central stone in an arch that holds the entire structure together. If removed, the arch collapses. Similarly, in DevRel teams, what we might call a "keystone team member" becomes essential to the organization's functioning—creating risk for both the individual and the team.

The keystone pattern develops gradually, often unintentionally. Someone with deep expertise takes on a critical responsibility. They handle it well, so they continue handling it. Documentation gets deferred because they're "too busy" executing. Before long, essential processes, relationships, or technical knowledge exist primarily in one person's head. When that person becomes unavailable—whether through vacation, illness, departure, or simply being overwhelmed—the team's function grinds to a halt.

What makes keystoning particularly insidious is that it often feels like success from the inside. The individual becomes highly valued, seemingly indispensable. Their expertise appears to provide job security. But this creates a trap for everyone involved. The individual becomes constrained by their own indispensability, unable to grow into new challenges because the team can't function without them. The team operates under constant risk, one absence away from crisis. The organization builds fragility into its operations, with critical capabilities depending entirely on a single individual.

The goal isn't eliminating expertise or individual excellence—those remain valuable. The goal is ensuring that expertise and capability are distributed across the team through intentional knowledge sharing and system building. When knowledge flows freely and multiple team members can handle critical functions, both individuals and teams become more resilient and capable of growth.

Recognizing Keystone Patterns

The keystone pattern appears in several forms across DevRel teams. Sometimes it's technical knowledge concentrated in one person's head. Other times, it's relationships that only one person can activate. Occasionally, it's process knowledge that hasn't been documented. The common thread is dependency—the team can't function effectively without a specific individual.

Common keystone patterns include

- **The Technical Expert:** Only one person deeply understands a particular area, with documentation existing primarily in their head.

- **The Relationship Holder:** Critical community or internal relationships depend on a single team member.
- **The Process Wizard:** Essential workflows rely on undocumented knowledge held by one person.
- **The Content Engine:** One team member produces a disproportionate amount of content.

These patterns might initially seem like individual achievements, but they create significant risk when that person becomes unavailable or leaves the organization. The goal isn't to eliminate expertise or excellence—it's to ensure that expertise and relationships distribute across the team through intentional knowledge sharing and system building.

Building Resilient Systems

Addressing keystone dependencies requires deliberate system building. It's not enough to recognize the pattern—you need to create structures and processes that distribute knowledge, relationships, and capability across the team. This work rarely feels urgent, which is why it often gets deferred until a crisis forces action.

Create comprehensive documentation of processes, relationships, and technical knowledge. Establish regular knowledge-sharing sessions within the team. Develop standard operating procedures that don't rely on individual expertise. Documentation shouldn't be perfect— "good enough" documentation created today is infinitely more valuable than the comprehensive guide you'll write someday.

Assign primary and secondary owners to key responsibilities and systems. Create multiple connection points for meaningful relationships. Implement paired approaches for critical functions. Distributed ownership means no single person becomes a bottleneck, and the team maintains function even when individuals are unavailable.

Recognize and reward knowledge sharing and system building. Allocate dedicated time for documentation and knowledge transfer. Define success to include team capability building alongside individual contribution. Cultural reinforcement makes system building a priority rather than something people do "when they have time."

These approaches create resilient teams that can maintain function even when key individuals are unavailable while allowing team members to focus on high-value contributions rather than maintaining "indispensable" status.

Managing Team Bandwidth

DevRel work is essentially unbounded—there's always more content to create, another event to attend, or another relationship to nurture. Teams inevitably stretch too thin without deliberate bandwidth management, reducing quality and risking burnout. The challenge isn't just managing current workload—it's creating sustainable practices that prevent chronic overload.

Setting Sustainable Expectations

Sustainable teams operate from explicit capacity models rather than reacting to incoming demands. Create explicit models for team capacity that account for all work types, including preparation and "invisible" work; allocate time realistically across priorities; and reserve capacity for unexpected opportunities. Most teams significantly underestimate the time required for preparation and coordination work.

Develop frameworks for declining or deferring requests that align decisions with strategic priorities, provide constructive alternatives when possible, and explain rationales clearly and respectfully. The ability to say no thoughtfully—and help requesters understand why—prevents the accumulation of commitments that eventually overwhelm the team.

Practical Bandwidth Management

Beyond setting expectations, implement practical approaches to maintain sustainable workloads. The "Drop, Defer, Delegate" framework provides a systematic approach to managing requests and commitments. Drop activities that don't align with strategic priorities or deliver sufficient value. Defer valuable initiatives that aren't right for the current moment. Delegate responsibilities that could be handled by other team members or functions. This framework makes prioritization explicit and creates space for strategic work.

Build intentional recovery periods into team operations through post-event recovery time, reduced expectations following intense project periods, and team "focus weeks" with minimal external commitments. Recovery integration prevents the normalization of overload while maintaining strategic focus.

These practices prevent the normalization of overload while maintaining strategic focus.

Creating a Culture of Continued Learning

The most effective DevRel teams prioritize continuous learning at individual and team levels. This learning orientation encompasses product expertise, professional skills development, and operational improvements that enhance team effectiveness and member satisfaction. In a field evolving as rapidly as Developer Relations, creating a learning culture isn't just beneficial—it's essential for long-term effectiveness.

Dual Learning Tracks: Product and Craft

Successful DevRel teams cultivate learning across two essential dimensions. Product and technology learning ensures your team maintains deep understanding of your platform's evolving capabilities, awareness of adjacent technologies in your ecosystem, knowledge of competitive solutions and alternatives, and familiarity with the broader industry landscape. This technical learning maintains the credibility that makes DevRel effective.

Professional growth and craft mastery develops communication and presentation skills, content creation and storytelling techniques, community building and management approaches, and strategic thinking and business acumen. These professional skills amplify technical knowledge into real impact.

This balanced learning approach ensures that team members remain technically credible while developing the professional skills that amplify their impact.

Learning Systems and Practices

Embed learning into your team's regular operations through structured approaches. Allocate protected hours for exploration and skill development; create learning budgets for courses, books, and conferences; and develop internal learning resources specific to your context. Dedicated learning time signals that growth is a priority, not something that happens only when other work is complete.

Establish regular tech talks and skill workshops, document insights and discoveries, create mentorship and peer learning programs, and facilitate cross-training in specialized areas. Knowledge-sharing mechanisms transform individual learning into team capability.

Regularly evaluate new tools that could enhance productivity, test process improvements in controlled environments, share successes and failures transparently, and implement promising approaches team-wide. Tool and process experimentation ensures your team continuously improves how you work, not just what you know.

These systematic practices transform learning from an occasional activity into a core team capability.

Learning Cycles

Effective learning happens across multiple timeframes, each serving different purposes. Ad hoc learning captures event-driven insights through post-event retrospectives, after-action reviews following major releases or launches, spontaneous learning sessions addressing emerging needs, and quick debriefs after significant community interactions. These event-driven moments capture fresh insights before they fade, turning experiences into actionable knowledge.

Regular learning rhythms establish consistent patterns through one-on-one coaching conversations that include learning goals, team learning sessions on rotating topics, monthly deep dives into specific technologies or skills, and regular reviews of content performance and community engagement. These consistent touchpoints focus on continuous improvement and prevent learning from being displaced by urgent demands.

Quarterly learning integration creates a structured review of learning patterns and insights, integration of discoveries into formal processes and approaches, revision of learning priorities based on emerging needs, and planning for skill development in upcoming quarters. These quarterly cycles connect individual learning to team capabilities and strategic priorities.

Long-term learning vision shapes comprehensive assessment of evolving skill requirements, identification of emerging technologies requiring expertise, development of long-term learning road maps, and strategic capability building aligned with company direction. These extended cycles ensure learning isn't merely reactive but anticipates future needs.

By integrating these learning cycles, DevRel teams develop resilience, adaptability, and ever-increasing effectiveness in serving developer communities and business objectives.

DevRel Leadership Evolution

Leading a Developer Relations team requires more than technical expertise or communication skills. As teams and organizations mature, the demands of DevRel leadership evolve significantly, requiring leaders to develop new capabilities while maintaining the foundational understanding that makes DevRel unique.

This evolution isn't simply about managing larger teams or broader responsibilities—it represents a fundamental shift in how DevRel leaders contribute value. Recognizing and navigating these transitions is essential for personal leadership development and organizational effectiveness.

The most successful DevRel leaders embrace this evolution, seeing each stage as an opportunity to expand their impact rather than departing from the hands-on work that initially drew them to the field. By understanding these developmental stages, current and aspiring DevRel leaders can chart a more intentional growth path.

From Technical Expert to Program Builder

Most DevRel leaders begin as exceptional individual contributors—advocates, content creators, or community builders with deep technical knowledge and strong communication skills. Their initial leadership opportunity often comes from this demonstrated excellence. However, the transition to leading programs requires a significant shift in focus and capabilities.

This transition requires moving from personal execution to system design—building frameworks and processes that others can execute, rather than delivering exceptional individual contributions. It means shifting from capability demonstration to capability development: helping team members develop their skills and effectiveness, rather than showcasing personal technical prowess. Leaders must embrace strategic prioritization over tactical excellence, making hard choices about where to invest limited resources rather than trying to do everything well. And they need to develop cross-functional influence instead of relying on direct control, building alignment and support across organizational boundaries rather than directly controlling outcomes.

This transition challenges many new DevRel leaders, as the skills and approaches that made them successful individual contributors don't directly translate to program leadership. Common struggles include difficulty delegating work they could do themselves (often faster or better), reluctance to invest time in "invisible" planning and coordination work, challenges articulating the strategic value of DevRel beyond activity metrics, and frustration with the slower pace of system building vs. individual delivery.

Successful navigation of this transition typically requires deliberate skill development, mentorship, and a willingness to embrace discomfort as new leadership muscles develop.

From Program Builder to Organizational Leader

As DevRel functions mature and expand, leadership requirements evolve further. Success now demands organizational leadership capabilities that extend far beyond DevRel-specific expertise. Strategic integration means aligning DevRel with broader business objectives and connecting developer success to organizational outcomes. Organizational design involves creating teams, structures, and processes that scale effectively across products, regions, and developer segments. Resource advocacy requires securing and allocating resources based on strategic priorities and measurable impact. Leadership development builds a pipeline of future leaders who can scale DevRel's impact beyond their span of control.

This stage of leadership involves thinking beyond DevRel as a function to how developer perspectives integrate throughout the organization. Rather than building excellent DevRel programs, these leaders shape how the company engages with developers.

This evolution requires mindset shifts and skill development, which are often supported by leadership training, executive coaching, and cross-functional experiences.

Building Leadership Distribution

Beyond developing individual leaders, creating distributed leadership capability throughout the team ensures sustainable scaling. Implement tiered responsibility levels with progressively increasing scope, create project and program leadership roles separate from management paths, rotate leadership opportunities across team members, and recognize and reward leadership contribution regardless of formal role.

This distributed approach transforms DevRel from a function dependent on exceptional individuals to an organizational capability that can scale and evolve.

TEAM STRUCTURE CHECK-IN

Grab a napkin (or open a doc) and spend 45 minutes getting honest about whether your team structure actually serves your strategy. This isn't about reorganizing everything—it's about identifying the friction points that are quietly draining your team's effectiveness.

Start by writing down your team's primary strategic objectives for the next year. Then list each team member's role and their main responsibilities.

Now comes the important part: draw lines connecting roles to objectives.

Where do you see gaps—objectives with no clear owner?

Where do you see pileups—one person connected to too many critical objectives?

Ask yourself:

- Which roles feel misaligned with what we're actually trying to accomplish?
- Where are we experiencing bottlenecks that slow down progress?
- What's one small structural adjustment that could unlock disproportionate impact?

The goal isn't creating the perfect org chart. It's identifying the highest-leverage structural changes—the ones that will reduce friction and let your team focus on work that matters. Share your findings with the team before making any changes. Often, the gaps you see from a leadership perspective look different from the ground level, and that perspective matters.

Conclusion: The Intentionally Designed DevRel Team

Building a DevRel team that operates effectively six months or a year from now requires making choices today that often feel counterintuitive. You hire for potential rather than perfect fit. You invest time documenting processes instead of just executing them. You distribute critical responsibilities even though it's faster to keep doing them yourself. You create systems that feel like overhead until the moment they prevent a crisis.

This intentional design transforms individual excellence into collective capability. The frameworks in this chapter—thoughtful team structures, strategic hiring, effective work distribution, resilience building, and continuous learning—all address a fundamental challenge: DevRel work is inherently unbounded, making it particularly vulnerable to burnout, overextension, and dependence on heroic individual efforts. Sustainable teams require deliberate systems that distribute work appropriately, prevent single points of failure, and create space for both execution and growth.

What makes this particularly challenging is that DevRel leadership requires navigating multiple tensions simultaneously: balancing technical excellence with organizational impact, managing creative flexibility within scalable processes, and developing both individual capability and team resilience. The most effective DevRel leaders don't resolve these tensions—they learn to hold them productively, making intentional choices about when to emphasize which side based on context and need.

Your team structure isn't a problem to solve once and forget. It's a living system that needs ongoing attention and adjustment as your organization grows, your platform evolves, and your team members develop. The goal isn't creating the perfect static organization—it's building a learning system that continuously improves its ability to serve both developers and the business while creating sustainable, meaningful work for the people doing it.

CHAPTER 13

Preparing for DevRel's Future

You've felt it before—that sinking sensation when a major industry shift catches you flat-footed. Maybe it was the explosion of large language models, or a framework that suddenly went from niche to ubiquitous, or a platform architecture that became the new standard seemingly overnight. You weren't alone in missing it. In conversations with DevRel leaders across the industry, nearly everyone describes the same struggle: being perpetually stuck in reactive mode, responding to business decisions that themselves are reactions to industry changes that were visible months earlier to those who were looking.

The problem isn't a lack of intelligence or dedication. It's that most DevRel leaders struggle to see beyond the next six months. They're drowning in the immediate demands of their road map, firefighting urgent issues, and scrambling to support the latest product launch. This creates a vicious cycle where you're always reacting to the business reacting to the industry, rather than positioning yourself as an expert who can guide your company into the future.

This chapter addresses a fundamental capability gap in DevRel: the ability to operate across multiple time horizons simultaneously, extract meaningful signals from overwhelming noise, and leverage emerging technologies to amplify rather than replace your expertise. These aren't separate skills—they form an integrated approach to strategic positioning that transforms DevRel from a perpetually reactive function into a forward-looking strategic asset.

The Time Horizon Framework

The most effective DevRel leaders live in multiple futures simultaneously. They're not just managing today's work; they're actively thinking about and preparing for what's coming in 12, 18, even 24 months. It's about deliberate time allocation that prevents you from being blindsided by shifts you should have anticipated.

K. Kemple, *Effective DevRel*, https://doi.org/10.1007/979-8-8688-2373-2_13

Think about how you currently spend your time. If you're like most DevRel professionals, nearly all your energy goes into what's directly in front of you: this quarter's content calendar, next month's event, this week's product launch, or today's crisis. These immediate demands are real and important. But when you operate exclusively in the present, you sacrifice your ability to shape the future.

A more strategic approach requires distributing your attention across different time horizons:

- Five percent of your time thinking about eighteen to twenty-four months out.
- Ten percent focused on twelve to eighteen months.
- Twenty percent considering six to twelve months.
- Sixty-five percent navigating the reality immediately in front of you—the next six months.

Five percent invested in the furthest horizon—just a few hours each month—creates enormous leverage by giving you time to position yourself as an expert in emerging areas before they become urgent priorities.

Why Time Horizons Matter

Decision-making today requires an understanding of where things are heading two to three years out. When you're evaluating which content to create, which partnerships to pursue, which technical areas to develop expertise in, or which developer needs to prioritize, you're not just serving today's developers—you're setting up the conditions for future success or failure.

Consider the cost of short-term thinking. When you only look six months ahead

- You miss the gradual shifts that compound into major changes.
- You invest in areas that are already declining.
- You fail to build relationships in communities that are gaining influence.
- You develop expertise in technologies that are being superseded.
- You forfeit your ability to guide your company's direction because you're always playing catch-up.

The alternative—operating across time horizons—creates strategic advantages that compound over time:

- You spot opportunities before your competitors.
- You build expertise in areas before they become crowded.
- You form relationships that position you as a trusted voice.
- You can advise your product and engineering teams about where developers are heading, not just where they are today.

These advantages transform your role from reactive executor to strategic partner.

Implementing Time Horizon Thinking

Living in multiple time horizons doesn't mean abandoning the present for speculation about the future. It means creating deliberate space for forward-thinking work within your existing responsibilities. The specific mechanisms vary based on your role and organization, but several patterns consistently work.

- **At the 18-to-24-month horizon:** Focus is on identifying fundamental shifts in developer expectations, technology paradigms, and ecosystem structure—understanding directional changes that will reshape your landscape. You're asking questions like: How are developers' workflows evolving? What new capabilities are becoming table stakes? Which technical approaches are gaining momentum in adjacent domains?
- **At 12 to 18 months:** Track specific trends that are starting to materialize. This is where you begin developing a point-of-view about what these shifts mean for your platform and community. You're starting conversations internally about what might need to change, identifying gaps in your current strategy, and potentially beginning to build expertise or relationships in these areas.
- **At 6 to 12 months:** Actively prepare for changes that are now quite visible. This is where forward-thinking work starts translating into concrete initiatives. You're planning content for emerging topics, proposing new technical approaches, establishing partnerships, or launching programs that will be fully relevant as these trends mature.

The key is making this thinking systematic rather than ad hoc. Block time in your calendar explicitly for longer-horizon thinking. Create a practice of reviewing and updating your understanding of these different timeframes. Share your observations with colleagues and stakeholders to refine your perspective and build organizational buy-in.

Extracting Signal from Noise

Information is not created equal, yet we often treat it as if it is. Your time, energy, and attention are your most valuable resources—far more finite than budget or headcount. The difference between reactive and strategic DevRel often comes down to your ability to filter the overwhelming volume of information flowing through your daily work and focus on what genuinely matters for your position in the industry.

Every day brings another blog post claiming to reveal the future, another framework promising to solve all your problems, or another hot take on what developers really want. Social media amplifies the noise, creating echo chambers where the same surface-level insights circulate endlessly while genuinely important signals get buried. Conference talks and vendor pitches add to the cacophony. Without a systematic approach to filtering this flood, you end up reactive—responding to whatever seems loudest rather than what actually matters.

Resilient Information Processes

The solution isn't trying to consume everything—that's a recipe for burnout and superficial understanding. Instead, you need resilient processes that automatically filter noise and surface signal. This starts with being ruthlessly clear about what you're trying to understand and why it matters.

Think about the information landscape as terrain you need to map. You're not trying to examine every tree and rock—you're identifying the major geographical features that will shape movement and settlement patterns. This metaphor applies directly to technology ecosystems: you're mapping the fundamental structures that will channel developer behavior and industry evolution.

To do this effectively, you need to look at longer time horizons than most of your peers. While others are obsessing over this quarter's trends, you're tracking multi-year trajectories. This longer view naturally filters out noise because most noise is time-sensitive—it seems urgent today but vanishes tomorrow. Signals, in contrast, persist and strengthen over time. By focusing on longer horizons, you automatically prioritize information with genuine strategic relevance.

Building Your Intelligence System

Understanding where the industry is heading and filtering signal from noise requires more than good intentions—it requires a systematic approach to gathering and synthesizing information from both internal and external sources. This isn't about complicated frameworks or elaborate processes. It's about consistently doing specific activities that give you visibility into what matters.

Internal Intelligence

Your own organization is one of your richest sources of forward-looking information, yet many DevRel professionals remain surprisingly disconnected from internal strategic thinking. The product road map, engineering team priorities, and executive strategy discussions contain crucial signals about where your company is positioning itself. These internal directions interact with external industry trends to create the specific context in which you need to operate.

Effective internal intelligence gathering involves specific activities:

- Embedding with product and engineering teams by attending their planning meetings to understand their thinking about market direction and technical evolution
- Attending internal enablement and demo sessions to learn context about why decisions were made and what alternatives were considered
- Doing deep research on internal projects, even ones that seem tangential, to understand the strategic bets your company is making
- Asking questions not just about what's being built, but why and what assumptions underlie these decisions

When engineering teams are excited about a particular technical approach or architectural pattern, they're often responding to broader industry movements that haven't fully materialized yet. Your job is to connect these internal signals to external trends.

External Intelligence

While internal intelligence tells you where your company is heading, external intelligence reveals where the industry is actually going. The gap between these two—when it exists—represents either opportunity or risk, depending on how you respond to it. Effective external intelligence gathering means deliberately building a network and information flow that gives you access to leading indicators.

Build your external intelligence through

- Going to industry events to understand what problems developers are actually struggling with and where community energy is flowing—pay attention to hallway conversations and Q&A sessions
- Building a network that gives you access to diverse perspectives—connecting with developers at companies that use your platform differently, engaging with adjacent communities, maintaining relationships with people who think differently
- Becoming a trusted leader yourself so information flows toward you—when you consistently provide value, people share what they're seeing and ask your opinion on emerging trends

The value of your network isn't its size—it's the diversity of perspectives and the quality of information flow.

Tracking What Actually Matters

With both internal and external intelligence sources established, you need to focus your attention on specific categories of information that will genuinely influence your strategic positioning. This is where many DevRel professionals get lost in abstraction or overwhelmed by volume. The solution is being concrete about what you're tracking and why it matters.

For example, if you work in the AI space, you might track

- Latest advancements in large language models—not every paper, but fundamental capability improvements that change what's possible and, more importantly, how these surface in user experience.
- Which categories of AI applications are getting the most traction—are coding assistants maturing faster than autonomous agents? Are RAG applications finding product-market fit better than fine-tuned models?
- Which tools or APIs get the balance right between utility, developer experience, and security—understanding why certain approaches succeed helps you advise your product teams.

The specific topics you track depend on your domain, but the principle remains constant: focus on understanding your actual operating environment and where that landscape is heading, not on tracking everything that might possibly matter. This focus is what separates useful intelligence from overwhelming noise.

Synthesizing into Action

Gathering information is only valuable if you can synthesize it into an actionable understanding. This synthesis is where the real strategic work happens—connecting internal and external intelligence to identify gaps, opportunities, and risks that should shape your priorities.

Create a simple tracking system that works for you. This doesn't need to be sophisticated—a document where you capture key observations, a periodic review process where you connect related signals, or regular conversations with stakeholders where you share what you're seeing. The mechanism matters less than the consistency.

Establish a review cadence aligned with your time horizons:

- **Weekly:** Review what's happening in the immediate 6-month window.
- **Monthly:** Step back to consider 6-to-12-month trends.
- **Quarterly:** Examine the 12-to-18-month landscape.
- **Annually:** Map out your understanding of the 18-to-24-month future.

This rhythm ensures you're regularly connecting new information to your existing understanding. Sharing your insights across the organization serves multiple purposes: it helps you refine your thinking through feedback, positions you as someone who understands industry direction, and creates shared context that makes your future-focused proposals more credible.

Counterintuitive AI Integration

As artificial intelligence capabilities expand rapidly, most guidance about using AI in DevRel misses the mark entirely. The typical advice—use AI to write your blog posts, generate your documentation, or create your presentations—leads to generic, voiceless content that diminishes rather than enhances your strategic value. Effective AI integration requires a fundamentally different approach.

The Wrong Approach

Let's be direct about what doesn't work. Using AI to generate finished artifacts undermines the very expertise that makes you valuable. When you prompt AI to generate complete work products, you're outsourcing the activities that establish your credibility and develop your understanding.

Avoid using AI for

- Writing your blog posts—they need your voice, your experiences, your specific insights from working with developers in your domain
- Building your demo applications—they need your understanding of what developers will struggle with and what shortcuts they'll try
- Creating your presentations—they need your storytelling, your ability to read a room, your strategic emphasis on what matters most

Beyond producing inferior work, this approach teaches you nothing. You don't develop deeper expertise. You don't discover new insights through the creative process. You don't build the judgment that comes from struggling with how to explain something clearly. You've outsourced not just the work but also the learning.

The Right Approach

Effective AI integration starts with a completely different question: What are the specific pain points, toil, and repetitive tasks in your workflow where AI could actually solve a problem that frees up your capacity for high-value work? The key is identifying narrow, concrete use cases where AI handles the garbage work that drains your time and energy without creating value.

Consider these effective AI applications:

- **NOT** "close my GitHub issues" **BUT** "categorize my GitHub issues and surface the most important based on these specific criteria"—you still make the decisions but work from organized information
- **NOT** "build me a website" **BUT** "generate custom Block Kit examples based on these other examples"—you maintain creative control while eliminating repetitive coding
- Converting content from one format to another—taking your conference talk transcript and transforming it into a base written article structure saves hours of mechanical work that you can then polish up
- Solving blank canvas problems—having AI generate a first-pass outline based on API specifications gives you something to improve rather than starting from nothing
- Attempting problems you wouldn't tackle without AI—analyzing patterns across hundreds of forum posts might surface insights you'd miss manually

Notice the pattern? AI handles tedious, mechanical work while you maintain strategic control and apply your expertise to the outputs.

Learning Faster and Working Smarter

Beyond handling toil, AI dramatically accelerates certain types of learning and research that expand your capabilities. These applications support genuine learning rather than substituting for it:

- Deep research on complex topics becomes more tractable when you can quickly iterate on questions and synthesize information across sources.
- Creating flashcards for technical concepts transforms passive reading into active recall practice.
- Generating practice problems or quizzes based on documentation reinforces your understanding.
- Qualitative interviewing—using AI to conduct structured interviews that extract expertise and tacit knowledge from subject matter experts, including yourself.

This last application—qualitative interviewing—represents one of the most powerful uses of AI in DevRel. The AI asks follow-up questions, probes for specifics, and identifies gaps in reasoning that you might miss when simply writing. This approach surfaces insights that remain buried in unstructured note-taking or stream-of-consciousness drafting.

What You Do with Freed Capacity

The entire point of using AI to handle toil and accelerate learning is creating capacity for work that genuinely requires your expertise, judgment, and creativity. This is where effective AI integration creates a strategic advantage rather than just marginal efficiency gains.

With the time you've freed up, you create those finished artifacts yourself—the blog posts that share your hard-won insights, the demos that showcase the elegant approaches you've discovered, and the presentations that tell compelling stories about where your platform fits in the evolving landscape. This work is where you build your reputation, develop your expertise, and create genuine value for developers.

You invest in strategic thinking that positions your team for the future. You can actually spend that 5% of your time on 18-24-month thinking because you're not drowning in mechanical tasks. You build relationships that create strategic options because you have the capacity for long conversations that develop mutual understanding.

You create higher-quality work because you're not exhausted from handling all the supporting tasks manually. Your blog posts are better because you've spent your energy on insight and storytelling rather than formatting and reorganization. Your demos are more thoughtful because you've had time to really consider what developers will struggle with. Your presentations are more compelling because you've focused on narrative rather than slide mechanics.

This is the counterintuitive insight that most AI guidance misses: AI's value isn't in replacing your expertise but in eliminating the obstacles that prevent you from fully applying it. The teams that master this distinction will build strategic advantages that compound over time, while those that use AI to outsource expertise will find themselves increasingly replaceable.

MAPPING YOUR STRATEGIC FUTURE

Understanding the concepts in this chapter is valuable, but only if you translate that understanding into specific actions for your situation. This exercise helps you assess your current state and develop a concrete plan for implementing time horizon thinking in your work.

Audit Your Time Allocation

Begin by honestly evaluating how you currently distribute your time and attention across different time horizons. For the past month, approximately what percentage of your time did you spend thinking about and working on initiatives at each time horizon? Be realistic—most people discover they're spending less than one percent on anything beyond six months out.

Now compare your current allocation to the target distribution: 5% at 18–24 months, 10% at 12–18 months, 20% at 6–12 months, and 65% on the immediate 6 months ahead. The gaps you identify reveal where you need to make changes in how you structure your time.

Identify Industry Trends

List five to seven specific trends or shifts in your industry that could impact your platform or community over the next 18–24 months. These should be concrete enough that you could track their progress, but significant enough that they would materially change how you approach your work if they fully materialize.

For each trend, note what signals you would watch to track its progression, which aspects of your current strategy might need adjustment if the trend accelerates, and what expertise or relationships you should start building now to position yourself effectively. This list becomes your working map of the future landscape—something you'll revisit and refine regularly.

Conclusion: Strategic Positioning vs. Perpetual Reaction

The DevRel leaders who master the capabilities in this chapter operate fundamentally differently than their peers. They're not smarter or harder-working—they've simply built systematic practices that prevent them from being trapped in perpetual reaction mode. They've created space for strategic thinking. They've developed processes that filter signal from noise. They've learned to use AI as a capacity multiplier rather than an expertise replacement.

The alternative—remaining focused exclusively on the immediate six months—leads inevitably back to the random acts of DevRel that this book has warned against. When you're always reacting to the business reacting to the industry, your work becomes disconnected from genuine developer needs or business impact. You're busy but not strategic. You're producing output but not building an advantage.

Being reactive and short-term focused doesn't just make your work harder—it makes you less valuable. When you can't advise your organization about where developers are heading, when you miss emerging opportunities that were visible to those looking ahead, or when you're blindsided by changes you should have anticipated, your influence diminishes. You become a tactical executor rather than a strategic partner.

The teams that invest in longer time horizon thinking, that build robust intelligence systems, and that use AI thoughtfully to amplify their expertise will find themselves increasingly essential to their organizations. They'll be the ones guiding their companies into the future rather than scrambling to catch up. They'll be the ones who spot opportunities early, build expertise before spaces become saturated, and maintain the strategic positioning that separates truly valuable DevRel from random acts of marketing disguised as developer relations.

The choice isn't between working on today's priorities or tomorrow's possibilities—it's about building the discipline to do both simultaneously. Five percent of your time thinking eighteen to twenty-four months out might seem like an impossible luxury when you're drowning in immediate demands. But that 5%—consistently applied—is what separates reactive execution from strategic leadership. It's what ensures that two years from now, you're positioned where you need to be rather than wondering how you missed what was always visible to those who were looking.

DevRel Frameworks and Worksheets

These comprehensive frameworks provide practical guidance for common DevRel challenges. Each framework includes an overview of the model, practical application guidelines, a real-world example, and reflective insights for implementation.

K. Kemple, *Effective DevRel*, https://doi.org/10.1007/979-8-8688-2373-2

APPENDIX A

YAP (Yet Another Program)

Model Overview

The YAP (Yet Another Program) mental model illustrates a critical inflection point that cross-functional teams face as they scale. The model is built on five core concepts:

- **Cross-functional competency requirement:** DevRel roles demand broader skill sets than specialized positions. Professionals must work effectively across multiple departments and stakeholder groups, requiring competencies that extend beyond a single functional area.
- **Alignment necessity:** Success depends heavily on alignment with other teams and departments. As the scope of work expands, the need for cross-functional alignment increases proportionally, creating additional coordination overhead.
- **Program management inflation:** Each new initiative requires additional management overhead, including documentation, workflows, synchronization meetings, and organizational tools. This overhead grows faster than the value delivered by the programs themselves.

K. Kemple, *Effective DevRel*, https://doi.org/10.1007/979-8-8688-2373-2

- **The inflection point:** There exists a critical threshold where the number of programs becomes counterproductive. Beyond this point, teams spend more time managing programs than actively participating in them or delivering value to developers.
- **Inverse productivity relationship:** As the number of programs increases beyond the inflection point, overall output and program success tend to decrease despite increased activity. Teams become so busy managing coordination that actual execution suffers.

The pattern follows a predictable cycle: opportunity identification leads to program creation, which shows initial success, generating expansion pressure from stakeholders. This creates operational strain as the team struggles to maintain quality across growing programs, resulting in execution inconsistency where programs receive uneven attention. The end result is impact dilution, where overall effectiveness decreases despite increased activity.

Application

To counter YAP syndrome, DevRel teams must shift from an opportunity-driven approach to an operations-first mindset. The goal isn't to do fewer things—it's to create systems that allow you to do more things with greater consistency and lower overhead.

Move from Traditional Program Management to Program Architecture: Traditional program management relies on custom processes for each program where success depends on specific program managers' approaches and knowledge lives primarily with key individuals. Program architecture uses standardized templates and frameworks where success depends on well-designed systems and processes, knowledge is embedded in documentation and workflows, and scaling happens through system optimization rather than just team growth.

Build scalable program foundations with three core elements:

1. **Repeatable:** Create consistent processes that maintain quality across all programs.
2. **Teachable:** Develop well-documented workflows that anyone can learn and execute.
3. **Measurable:** Implement clear metrics that demonstrate impact and allow for optimization.

Separate program management from program participation by designating specific roles for program strategy, logistics coordination, stakeholder relationships, and cross-program measurement. This separation allows specialists to focus on their core expertise—content creation, technical delivery, developer relationships, and domain-specific insights—rather than being pulled into operational overhead.

Implement operational systems that scale alongside your team's growth. Create centralized content libraries that ensure consistency in messaging across all channels. Establish structured feedback pipelines that capture insights from various sources and route them to the right stakeholders for action. Develop tiered approaches to programs with clear processes for each tier, ensuring that high-touch and low-touch initiatives receive appropriate levels of attention. Leverage automation for routine tasks, notifications, and distribution to free up your team's time for higher-value work.

Reflection

The YAP model reveals that growth without operational discipline leads to decreased effectiveness. Many DevRel leaders mistakenly interpret increased activity as increased impact, failing to recognize when program management overhead has exceeded the value programs deliver.

The most successful teams recognize that their value lies in the quality of their engagement and the depth of their insights, not just the volume of their output. Operational excellence isn't about efficiency for its own sake—it's about creating the conditions where your team's expertise can actually make a difference.

Consider regularly assessing your team's ratio of program management time to program participation time. If your advocates spend more time coordinating programs than actually talking to developers, creating content, or gathering insights, you've crossed the YAP inflection point. The solution isn't to eliminate programs—it's to architect them for scale from the beginning.

APPENDIX B

Drop, Defer, Delegate Model

Model Overview

The Drop, Defer, Delegate framework provides a structured approach for making intentional decisions about where to invest limited resources. When faced with more opportunities than capacity, many DevRel teams attempt everything—working longer hours, sacrificing quality, or burning out team members. This framework offers a healthier alternative.

Drop: The Courage to Say No

Dropping activities requires acknowledging that not everything represents the best use of your limited resources, even if those activities have intrinsic value. The key is distinguishing between activities that feel productive and those that genuinely advance strategic priorities.

Candidates for dropping include low-alignment activities that don't directly support strategic priorities, and limited-impact efforts where the potential benefit doesn't justify the required investment. Consider dropping programs with diminishing returns—established activities whose effectiveness has declined over time. Look also at responsibilities that aren't really your job, functions that would be better owned by other teams. Finally, examine outdated traditions, activities maintained primarily because "we've always done them" rather than because they still deliver value.

K. Kemple, *Effective DevRel*, https://doi.org/10.1007/979-8-8688-2373-2

Defer: Strategic Timing of Initiatives

Deferring recognizes that many initiatives have genuine value but not necessarily at the present moment. Strategic deferral creates space for current priorities while preserving future opportunities.

Candidates for deferring include promising but premature initiatives—ideas with potential that depend on not-yet-established foundations. Some programs are sequencing-dependent and would be more effective after other work completes. Others are resource-constrained opportunities that require capabilities or bandwidth not currently available. You might also defer future-aligned priorities that will have greater relevance in upcoming product or business cycles, or good-but-not-urgent ideas that are valuable but don't address immediate strategic needs.

Delegate: Expanding Your Impact Through Others

Delegation recognizes that impact isn't limited to your direct work but includes what you enable others to accomplish. Effective delegation multiplies your team's capacity while developing capabilities across the organization.

Delegation opportunities include appropriate cross-functional work—activities better aligned with other teams' core responsibilities—and growth-enabling responsibilities that provide development opportunities for team members. Look for community contribution opportunities where engaged community members could effectively handle the work, or specialized execution that requires expertise your team doesn't need to maintain internally.

Finally, consider delegating operational tasks and routine activities that support resources could handle, freeing your team for higher-value work.

Reflection

The ability to prioritize effectively can be the difference between thriving and merely surviving. The Three D's framework provides a tool to cut through the noise and focus on what truly drives value for developers and the business.

The hardest part of this framework is often the dropping. We naturally want to say yes to everything, especially when we see the potential value. But saying yes to everything means saying no to depth, quality, and ultimately impact. Every yes is a no to something else—the question is whether you're making that choice intentionally or letting circumstances decide for you.

Consider that some of the best decisions you'll make are about what not to do. The projects you decline, the initiatives you defer, and the work you delegate all create space for the work that only you can do. When you're spread too thin, you're not just less effective—you're preventing your team from doing their best work too.

APPENDIX C

Pyramid of Challenge

Model Overview

The Pyramid of Challenge model addresses how vital the distribution of challenge is to a team's success. Challenge plays an essential role in happiness and retention—developers leave jobs either because the work is no longer challenging and there's no career growth, or because the work is too challenging and they have no support. Understanding this model helps you build teams that keep people engaged and growing.

Core Concept

The model uses a triangle representing a group's entire workload, where the x-axis represents the amount of work available and the y-axis represents the complexity of work available. Together they show that as work increases in complexity, it decreases in availability—you need only one or two people to architect an application, but many more to build it. This natural distribution of work complexity forms the foundation for thinking about team composition.

Three Levels of Work Complexity

The pyramid divides work into three distinct levels, each requiring different skills and experience:

1. **High complexity/low volume:** Architecture, systems design, strategic planning, measurement frameworks. This work requires extensive experience and systems thinking. Fewer people are needed for this level.

K. Kemple, *Effective DevRel*, https://doi.org/10.1007/979-8-8688-2373-2

2. **Medium complexity/medium volume:** Significant content creation, workshop development, program implementation, community program management. This work benefits from solid experience and specialized skills. Moderate staffing is needed.

3. **Low complexity/high volume:** Routine community engagement, content updates, event support, documentation maintenance. This work provides excellent learning opportunities for newer team members. More people are needed for this level.

Understanding these levels helps you identify where your team has capacity and where you might have gaps.

Common Team Imbalances

When team composition doesn't align with the work distribution, several predictable problems emerge:

- **Top-heavy distribution:** Too many senior members create a challenge gap at the bottom. Senior developers are forced to do less complex and more frequent tasks even though it's not challenging, leading to toiling. Teams could suffer from overly complex solutions, an inability to reach consensus, and high turnover as members leave to seek new challenges.
- **Bottom-heavy distribution:** A team without enough seniority or leadership suffers from a challenge gap at the top. Teams face a situation where they are overchallenged by not having the skills or experience needed to meet their responsibilities. Members are likely to suffer from burnout, and output could be brittle without proper guidance from experienced leaders.
- **Opposing distribution:** Teams with one or two very senior people and then more junior developers face a challenge gap at the center. Senior developers are forced to work on all non-challenging tasks that junior developers aren't capable of handling yet, while also trying to mentor them. This greatly impacts their ability to handle

their own responsibilities while other responsibilities get dropped or mishandled. Less experienced developers won't get the support they need and will often be tasked with work outside their current skill set.

- **Centered distribution:** Teams consisting of mid-level developers but lacking any really senior or junior developers create a challenge gap at each end. Teams are susceptible to infighting around responsibilities, looking for work that fits within their comfort zone. Some work could be too complex, causing fragility in solutions. Teams may be very process-heavy as members look for ways to contribute. Some members may try to step up and take on responsibilities that are too challenging, leading to burnout.

Recognizing these patterns in your own team is the first step toward addressing them.

Reflection

The Pyramid of Challenge model reveals that team composition isn't just about headcount—it's about matching people to work that appropriately challenges them. This model helps explain patterns you might be seeing in your team without understanding why.

If you're experiencing high turnover among senior team members, look at whether they're spending too much time on work below their capability level. If junior team members seem overwhelmed or burning out, examine whether they're being asked to handle complexity beyond their current skills. If your mid-level team members are fighting over responsibilities, you might have a centered distribution with gaps at both ends.

Remember that this model is a guide, not a rigid rule. Communication with your team is more important than any framework. Regular conversations about whether people feel appropriately challenged, supported, and able to grow are essential. The pyramid helps you structure those conversations and identify potential issues before they become serious problems.

The model also reminds us that career growth isn't always vertical. Sometimes the most valuable learning comes from taking on different types of challenges at the same complexity level, building breadth before depth, or rotating through different areas to understand the full picture. Use this framework as a starting point for deeper conversations about how to keep your team engaged and growing.

APPENDIX D

Keystone Model

Model Overview

The Keystone Model identifies and addresses single points of failure in teams. In traditional architecture, a keystone is the central stone in an arch that holds the entire structure together. If removed, the arch collapses. Similarly, in DevRel teams, a "keystone team member" becomes essential to the organization's functioning—creating risk for both the individual and the team.

A keystone is a team member who becomes essential to operations, creating risk when unavailable. The pattern develops gradually and often unintentionally. Someone with deep expertise takes on a critical responsibility, handles it well, and continues handling it. Documentation gets deferred because they're "too busy" executing. Before long, essential processes, relationships, or technical knowledge exist primarily in one person's head. Recognizing this pattern early is crucial to preventing the problems it creates.

Red Flags Indicating Keystone Patterns

Watch for these warning signs that someone is becoming a keystone in your organization:

1. **"I'll handle it" syndrome:** One team member consistently volunteers to take on crucial tasks because "it's just easier if I do it."
2. **Documentation black hole:** Processes exist only in someone's head, with little to no written guidance.

K. Kemple, *Effective DevRel*, https://doi.org/10.1007/979-8-8688-2373-2

3. **Knowledge hoarding:** Information is treated like a precious resource, doled out in small doses rather than shared freely.
4. **The indispensable one:** Team progress grinds to a halt when a specific person is unavailable.
5. **"It's complicated" excuse:** Explanations for how things work are consistently vague or overly complex, making knowledge transfer difficult.

If you notice multiple red flags around the same person, you likely have a keystone situation developing.

Common Keystone Patterns

Keystone dependencies manifest in several characteristic ways:

- **The Technical Expert:** Only one person deeply understands a particular area, with documentation existing primarily in their head.
- **The Relationship Holder:** Critical community or internal relationships depend on a single team member.
- **The Process Wizard:** Essential workflows rely on undocumented knowledge held by one person.
- **The Content Engine:** One team member produces a disproportionate amount of content, creating dependency.

Understanding which pattern you're facing helps you develop the right strategy to address it.

Why Keystoning Is Insidious

It often feels like success from the inside. The individual becomes highly valued, seemingly indispensable. Their expertise appears to provide job security. But this creates a trap for everyone involved.

The individual becomes constrained by their own indispensability, unable to grow into new challenges because the team can't function without them. The team operates under constant risk, one absence away from crisis. The organization builds fragility into its operations, with critical capabilities depending entirely on a single individual. What looks like strength is actually vulnerability in disguise.

Reflection

The keystone pattern is particularly dangerous because it rewards the behavior that creates it. Being the "go-to person" feels good. Being seen as indispensable can feel like job security. But it's a trap.

For the individual, being a keystone prevents growth. You can't take on new challenges when the team can't function without you in your current role. You can't take a real vacation. You can't be sick without causing problems. And paradoxically, while you feel indispensable, you're also preventing yourself from moving up—because who would replace you?

For the team, keystones create fragility. What happens when the keystone gets a better offer? Gets sick? Burns out from being constantly needed? The team faces a crisis that could have been prevented with proper knowledge distribution.

For the organization, keystones represent unmitigated risk. Critical capabilities shouldn't depend on any single person, no matter how talented. Resilient organizations build systems where expertise is shared, processes are documented, and anyone can be sick or take a vacation without creating crises.

The solution isn't to eliminate expertise—it's to distribute it. The goal is to ensure that knowledge flows freely and multiple team members can handle critical functions. When this happens, both individuals and teams become more resilient and capable of growth. True value isn't in being irreplaceable—it's in making everyone around you more capable.

APPENDIX E

Sentiment Inertia Index (Sii)

Model Overview

The Sentiment Inertia Index (Sii) is a predictive metric designed to quantify trapped user frustration in B2B SaaS. It measures the dangerous gap between poor customer sentiment and low churn, identifying situations where dissatisfied users are unable to leave due to switching costs, vendor lock-in, or organizational inertia. This metric helps you see the competitive vulnerability that traditional retention metrics often hide.

Formula

The Sentiment Inertia Index uses a simple but powerful calculation to reveal hidden risk:

$$\text{Sii} = (100 - \text{NPS}) / \text{Churn Rate}$$

where NPS is your Net Promoter Score (ranging from -100 to 100), measuring customer sentiment, and Churn Rate is your monthly customer or user attrition percentage.

The numerator (100 - NPS) creates a Dissatisfaction Score representing the amount of frustration or pressure building within the user base. The denominator Churn Rate represents the leakiness of the customer moat. A low churn rate contains the pressure, increasing disruption risk. Together, these components reveal how much frustration is being contained by your switching costs.

K. Kemple, *Effective DevRel*, https://doi.org/10.1007/979-8-8688-2373-2

Risk Scale

Understanding your Sii score requires knowing where it falls on the risk spectrum:

- **< 15 (Low risk):** High customer satisfaction is reinforced by strong retention. The user base is stable and happy.
- **15–35 (Guarded):** Satisfaction may be declining or mediocre, but the moat is largely intact. An early warning to investigate sentiment.
- **35–60 (Elevated):** Significant dissatisfaction is being contained by customer lock-in. Prime conditions for mass exodus if a compelling alternative appears.
- **> 60 (Critical):** Extreme user frustration is trapped. The user base is highly vulnerable to a competitor's arrival, especially through bottom-up adoption.

These thresholds help you understand not just where you stand today, but how urgently you need to act.

Real-World Calibration

Seeing how the Sii applies to real companies helps calibrate your understanding of the risk levels:

- **SAP/Oracle (~15 NPS, ~0.5% churn):** Sii = 170 (Critical)
- **Jira/Confluence (~35 NPS, ~1.5% churn):** Sii = 43 (Elevated)
- **Adobe pre-Figma (~40 NPS, ~1% churn):** Sii = 60 (Elevated)
- **Linear/Notion (~60 NPS, ~3% churn):** Sii = 13 (Low Risk)

These examples show how even well-known enterprise platforms can harbor significant competitive vulnerability.

Usage Notes

To get accurate and actionable results from the Sii, follow these guidelines:

1. **Align your metrics:** NPS and churn must measure the same population (enterprise NPS requires enterprise customer churn, user NPS requires user churn).
2. **Prioritize people metrics:** User/customer churn is more effective than revenue churn for measuring user frustration.
3. **Use a trending indicator:** A single Sii score is useful, but tracking over time provides a powerful early warning of sentiment collapse.
4. **High scores signal vulnerability:** Companies in the elevated or critical range are ripe for disruption through bottom-up competitor adoption.

Applied correctly, the Sii becomes an early warning system for competitive threats.

Reflection

The Sentiment Inertia Index reveals a dangerous pattern in B2B SaaS: stable usage with declining satisfaction is not a reassuring signal—it's the most dangerous pattern you can see. It means you have frustrated users who can't easily leave.

The rise of Product-Led Growth (PLG) has completely changed what happens when captive users reach their breaking point. When competitors offer free trials or freemium tiers, every frustrated user becomes a potential defector who can validate alternatives immediately. What used to take months of evaluation now happens in weeks or even days.

Traditional retention metrics can create a false sense of security. Teams look at low churn rates and assume everything is fine, not realizing that they're sitting on a pressure cooker of user frustration. The Sii makes this invisible risk visible, providing an early warning system for competitive vulnerability.

The most critical insight is that high Sii scores precede revenue impact by months or even years. By the time churn starts increasing, frustration coalitions have already formed and alternatives have been validated. The company has lost its chance to address the underlying issues proactively.

For DevRel teams, the Sii provides a powerful tool for advocating for developer experience improvements. When you can show leadership that your platform has a high Sii score, you're not just pointing out problems—you're quantifying competitive risk in a language executives understand.

Remember: NPS was designed to predict growth, but in B2B SaaS with high switching costs, it often doesn't correlate with churn. The Sii restores that predictive power by accounting for the "moat" that keeps unhappy customers trapped. When that moat eventually breaks—through PLG, through frustration coalitions, through any number of competitive disruptions—the exodus can be sudden and devastating.

APPENDIX F

Frustration Coalitions

Model Overview

A Frustration Coalition is an informal alliance of end-users within an organization who unite around shared dissatisfaction with an incumbent tool, ultimately driving organizational switching decisions. This framework draws from established theories in social sciences, organizational behavior, and diffusion research. Understanding how these coalitions form gives you the power to either prevent them in your own organization or catalyze them against competitors.

The Six-Stage Formation Process

Frustration coalitions don't emerge randomly—they follow a predictable progression from individual pain to collective action:

- **Stage 1. Individual friction:** Users encounter persistent pain points disrupting daily workflows, creating ongoing personal dissatisfaction. At this stage, problems feel individual—each person thinks they're the only one struggling or that something is wrong with their approach.
- **Stage 2. Collective recognition:** Multiple users begin to recognize frustrations as systemic and widespread rather than isolated personal experiences. The conversation shifts from "I'm having trouble with..." to "We're all struggling with..." This recognition catalyzes coalition formation.

K. Kemple, *Effective DevRel*, https://doi.org/10.1007/979-8-8688-2373-2

- **Stage 3. Alternative research:** Proactive individuals start exploring competitor solutions, sharing insights and comparisons within their networks. Someone becomes the unofficial "researcher" who investigates options and shares findings with colleagues.
- **Stage 4. Coalition formation:** An informal group solidifies around a specific competitor solution that directly addresses their frustrations. The coalition develops shared language, examples, and arguments for change.
- **Stage 5. Internal advocacy:** The coalition presents a cohesive, well-documented business case to organizational decision-makers, highlighting the benefits of switching. By this point, multiple team members have validated the alternative, creating social proof.
- **Stage 6. Switching decision:** Organizational leadership responds by choosing the path of least internal resistance—aligning with user preferences to resolve collective dissatisfaction. When enough employees advocate for change, leadership follows their lead to maintain productivity and morale.

Each stage builds momentum toward the next, making early intervention critical.

Scientific Foundations

The frustration coalition framework isn't just observational—it's grounded in decades of research on collective behavior and organizational change:

- Olson's "Logic of Collective Action" (1965) explains how individual grievances become collective concerns.
- Rogers' "Diffusion of Innovations" (1962) describes the progression from awareness to adoption.
- Kotter's "Leading Change" (1996) highlights the importance of internal coalitions for change.
- Granovetter's "Threshold Models" (1978) identifies tipping points in collective behavior.

These theoretical foundations validate what many practitioners have observed: user-driven change follows consistent, predictable patterns.

Reflection

Frustration coalitions reveal that B2B software buying decisions are increasingly bottom-up rather than top-down. The traditional enterprise sales model assumed decisions flowed from executives to users. PLG and modern work patterns have inverted this: users make decisions and executives formalize them.

This inversion creates both threat and opportunity. For incumbents, it means you can no longer rely on procurement friction and switching costs to protect your market position. When users are unhappy enough to form coalitions, they find ways around traditional barriers. The "moat" you thought you had turns out to be a dam—and dams eventually break under sufficient pressure.

For disruptors, understanding coalition formation provides a road map for market entry. Instead of trying to sell to executives who don't feel the pain, you arm frustrated users with tools to advocate for themselves. Make it easy for them to try your solution, validate it with colleagues, and present a unified case for change.

For DevRel teams, this framework should fundamentally change how you think about your role. You're not just advocates for developers—you're early warning systems for coalition formation. When you see similar complaints from multiple users, that's not just feedback to log—it's the beginning of a coalition that could lead to churn.

The most important insight is this: frustration coalitions don't form overnight, but once they reach critical mass, change happens fast. The time to address friction is before coalitions form, not after. By the time you're trying to prevent users from leaving, you've already lost—they're just waiting for the right alternative to appear.

APPENDIX G

90-Day Leadership Plan (Learn, Partner, Propose)

Model Overview

The 90-Day Leadership Plan provides a structured approach for new DevRel leaders to build understanding, form partnerships, and develop strategic recommendations. This framework recognizes that meaningful leadership requires deep context before proposing change. By dividing the first three months into distinct phases, the plan helps leaders resist premature action while building the credibility needed for lasting impact.

Core Structure: Three 30-Day Phases

The plan divides your first quarter into three progressive phases, each building on the previous one:

- **Days 1–30:** Learn & Observe - The first month focuses on building a deep understanding through active learning and observation without trying to change anything. This phase establishes technical foundation, ecosystem knowledge, and initial relationships.
- **Days 31–60:** Partner & Contribute - The second month shifts to active participation and contribution while continuing to learn. Leaders begin adding value through partnerships while gathering feedback on initial observations.

K. Kemple, *Effective DevRel*, https://doi.org/10.1007/979-8-8688-2373-2

- **Days 61–90:** Propose & Plan - The final month focuses on synthesizing learnings into actionable recommendations while maintaining a collaborative approach. Leaders present well-researched proposals based on deep context.

This phased approach ensures you earn credibility before attempting to drive change.

Key Principles Throughout

Seven guiding principles should inform your actions across all three phases:

1. **Focus on learning:** Maintain a learning mindset even when contributing.
2. **Build relationships:** Invest in genuine connections with team and partners.
3. **Stay curious:** Ask questions and seek to understand deeply.
4. **Add value:** Look for ways to contribute while learning.
5. **Document everything:** Keep detailed notes of observations and insights.
6. **Respect existing work:** Acknowledge and build upon current foundations.
7. **Stay humble:** Recognize that significant learning takes time.

Following these principles throughout the 90 days ensures you build trust while gathering the context you need.

Reflection

The 90-day plan's power comes from resisting the urge to demonstrate value through quick changes. New leaders often feel pressure to "make an impact" immediately, leading to proposals that lack context and alienate existing team members.

The Learn/Partner/Propose structure acknowledges that effective leadership requires earning the right to lead. You earn that right by demonstrating that you understand the context, respect existing work, and have invested in relationships. Only then do your proposals carry weight.

The hardest part is often the restraint required in the first month. You'll see things you want to change. You'll have ideas for improvements. You'll be tempted to propose changes to "prove" your value. Resist. The discipline of learning first makes your eventual proposals vastly more effective.

This framework is particularly valuable when joining organizations with strong existing cultures and successful track records. Your new perspective is valuable, but only when combined with deep contextual understanding. The 90-day structure ensures you build that understanding before trying to drive change.

For teams receiving new leaders, this framework sets appropriate expectations. Leaders who follow this approach signal respect for existing work and commitment to understanding before changing. This builds trust and creates psychological safety for honest feedback.

APPENDIX H

Gap-Filling Expertise

Model Overview

DevRel operates at the intersection of multiple disciplines—technical, marketing, product, legal, data, design. When cross-functional partners lack bandwidth to provide timely support, AI projects can help maintain momentum by bridging expertise gaps temporarily.

The Gap-Filling Expertise Model uses AI to simulate cross-functional expertise when specialist teams are at capacity. This isn't about replacing human collaboration—it's about maintaining progress and improving preparation for eventual expert engagement. The model recognizes that specialist bottlenecks are a reality of modern organizations and provides a structured way to work around them without sacrificing quality.

Key Applications

AI can provide gap-filling support across several critical functional areas:

1. **Data analysis support:** Creating initial SQL queries and metric frameworks when data teams are unavailable.

2. **Content review assistance:** Preliminary legal/PR reviews before human expert engagement.

3. **Design guidance:** Initial brand consistency feedback based on guidelines.

4. **Marketing strategy support:** Campaign ideas and distribution suggestions for content.

K. Kemple, *Effective DevRel*, https://doi.org/10.1007/979-8-8688-2373-2

These applications share a common thread: they help you make progress while waiting for specialist availability.

Value Proposition

Gap-filling expertise delivers several distinct benefits that go beyond simply working faster:

- Maintains momentum when cross-functional support is temporarily unavailable
- Improves preparation for expert collaboration by developing more refined drafts
- Expands capabilities in adjacent areas through structured learning
- Creates space for more strategic use of specialist time

When applied correctly, this approach transforms how you engage with specialist teams.

Critical Limitations

Understanding what this model cannot do is as important as knowing its strengths:

- **NOT** a replacement for actual cross-functional collaboration.
- Quality depends on input materials provided (guidelines, examples, documentation).
- Best used for initial drafts and brainstorming, not final decisions.
- Should always be followed up with actual expert review when the stakes are high.

Respecting these limitations ensures you use the model appropriately and avoid the pitfalls of over-reliance.

Example

At Slack, the DevRel team needed to create SQL queries for a new developer engagement dashboard. The data team was fully committed to a company-wide analytics migration for the next month. Rather than waiting or creating potentially incorrect queries, the team used gap-filling expertise.

The team assembled the materials they needed to simulate data analyst support. They uploaded database schema documentation, included examples of previous queries for similar metrics, and configured an AI project as a data analyst with context about Slack's data structure.

The team iteratively refined queries through multiple exchanges:

1. "Show me how to track unique developers creating apps per month."
2. AI generated the initial query using uploaded schemas.
3. Team tested the query and found it needed adjustment for workspace filtering.
4. "Adjust this query to filter only production workspaces."
5. AI refined the query with appropriate filters.

By the time the data team had bandwidth, the DevRel team had working queries that captured 80% of needed metrics, clear documentation of logic and assumptions, specific questions about edge cases requiring data team expertise, and a refined list of metrics that truly mattered.

The data team meeting became a strategic discussion about the 20% that needed expert input rather than starting from scratch. The engagement took 30 minutes instead of multiple hours, and the final dashboard launched two weeks earlier than it would have otherwise.

Critical Note The team always flagged queries as "preliminary pending data team review" and never made business decisions based solely on AI-generated analytics. The gap-filling was about maintaining momentum, not replacing expertise.

Reflection

The Gap-Filling Expertise Model acknowledges a reality of modern organizations: specialist teams are often at capacity, creating bottlenecks for dependent work. The traditional response is either waiting (losing momentum) or proceeding without expertise (risking quality).

This model offers a third path: use AI to bridge the gap temporarily, maintaining momentum while preparing for more effective specialist engagement. The keyword is "temporarily"—this is about gaps, not replacements.

The model works best when you have clear examples of what good looks like. AI can pattern-match against your brand guidelines, example queries, or approved content. It struggles when you lack that foundation. If you don't have documented guidelines or examples, your first step should be creating those—which is valuable regardless of AI usage.

There's an important psychological shift required: you're not asking AI to be the expert, you're using it to organize your thinking and create better inputs for the actual expert. The AI's value isn't in its answer—it's in forcing you to articulate what you need and providing a starting point for refinement.

The biggest risk is over-reliance. It's tempting to skip the expert review step when AI gives you something that looks reasonable. Resist this temptation. The model's value comes from making specialist collaboration more efficient, not from eliminating it. Always loop in actual experts before making high-stakes decisions or publishing customer-facing content.

APPENDIX I

Lava Leadership

Model Overview

Lava Leadership describes how strategic thinkers can drive organizational change from positions without formal authority. Like lava building pressure beneath the Earth's surface before bursting forth, strategic ideas can build momentum within an organization before breaking through and cascading from executive levels. This model recognizes that positional authority isn't required for strategic impact—what's required is evidence, coalitions, patience, and framing.

Just as lava forces its way through earth's layers when pressure builds sufficiently, ideas from lower levels of an organization can eventually erupt and flow from the top, reshaping the landscape when they build enough support and evidence. The key is understanding how to build that pressure strategically.

Key Challenges

Strategic thinkers without formal authority face several predictable obstacles when trying to drive organizational change:

1. **Multiple layers of approval:** Ideas must navigate through various management levels, each with own priorities.
2. **Limited visibility:** Lower-level employees struggle to get ideas in front of key decision-makers.

K. Kemple, *Effective DevRel*, https://doi.org/10.1007/979-8-8688-2373-2

3. **Resistance to change:** Established processes and cultures create inertia against new approaches.
4. **Time constraints:** Gaining buy-in can be slow, potentially allowing competitors to move ahead.

Understanding these challenges helps you develop strategies to overcome them systematically.

Strategies for Effective Lava Leadership

The Lava Leadership model requires building pressure through evidence, coalition-building, and strategic patience. Eight key strategies help you navigate this process:

1. **Build a coalition:** Start by finding allies at your level and in adjacent departments. The more support you can garner, the more credible your idea becomes as it moves up the chain.
2. **Speak the language of leadership:** Frame your ideas in terms of organizational goals, KPIs, and strategic priorities. Show how your proposal aligns with and advances the company's mission.
3. **Create a compelling narrative:** Craft a clear, concise story around your idea. Use data, case studies, and concrete examples to illustrate the potential impact.
4. **Leverage informal networks:** Utilize your connections across the organization to spread awareness of your idea and gather feedback. This can create a groundswell of support.
5. **Identify and cultivate executive sponsors:** Look for leaders who have shown openness to new ideas or who have a stake in the problem you're trying to solve. Nurture these relationships over time.
6. **Start small:** Consider piloting your idea on a smaller scale. Success in a limited context can provide powerful evidence for broader implementation.

7. **Be patient and persistent:** Remember that significant changes often take time. Stay committed to your vision while remaining open to feedback and iteration.
8. **Prepare for the eruption:** As your idea gains traction, be ready to support its implementation. Develop detailed plans and be prepared to take on a leadership role in bringing your vision to life.

These strategies work together to build the pressure needed for your ideas to break through organizational layers.

Reflection

Lava Leadership reveals an important truth about organizational change: positional authority isn't required for strategic impact. What's required is evidence, coalitions, patience, and framing.

The model works because it recognizes how organizations actually function. Change rarely happens through formal authority alone—it happens when multiple signals align: peer support, executive sponsorship, demonstrated value, and business case alignment.

The hardest part is the patience required. Eight months from idea to organization-wide adoption feels slow. You'll be tempted to push harder, escalate faster, and demand action. Resist. Like lava, rushing to the surface before building sufficient pressure leads to small eruptions that don't reshape the landscape.

The model also requires genuine humility. Your idea will change through the process. Feedback from coalitions, sponsors, and pilots will reveal blind spots. The final implemented version will look different from your original vision. That's not failure—it's strength. Ideas refined through diverse perspectives emerge stronger.

For individual contributors, Lava Leadership offers a path to impact that doesn't depend on promotion. You can drive strategic change from any position if you're willing to invest the effort in building cases, coalitions, and evidence.

For organizations, encouraging Lava Leadership creates a competitive advantage. The best strategic insights often come from people closest to problems—customers, products, processes. Organizations that tap into this thinking at all levels innovate faster and adapt more effectively.

The key is recognizing that formal authority and strategic leadership are different capabilities. Some people have both, but many strategic thinkers lack formal authority, and many people with authority lack strategic vision. Lava Leadership enables organizations to benefit from strategic thinking regardless of where it originates in the hierarchy.

APPENDIX J

Three R's (Recognition, Request, Reward)

Model Overview

The Three R's Model provides a framework for asking developers (or anyone) to participate, cooperate, or support your initiatives. The model creates mutual value rather than one-sided transactions, building sustainable relationships instead of exhausting goodwill.

All relationships are inherently transactional in the sense that they involve value exchange. The question isn't whether relationships are transactional—it's whether transactions create value for all parties or just one. This framework ensures your asks benefit everyone involved.

Three Components

The model breaks down effective requests into three essential elements that work together to create mutually beneficial exchanges:

1. **Recognition:** Acknowledge why you're asking this specific person. Identify their unique expertise or perspective, show you've thoughtfully selected them rather than mass-asking, demonstrate awareness of their specific contributions, and get consent even to make your request. This step shows respect for their time and establishes that your ask is intentional, not arbitrary.

K. Kemple, *Effective DevRel*, https://doi.org/10.1007/979-8-8688-2373-2

2. **Request:** Clearly state what you're asking for. Be specific about the scope of commitment, include a timeline and expected effort, make it easy to understand what they'd be agreeing to, and provide all necessary context for informed decision-making. Clarity here removes ambiguity and allows people to make confident decisions.

3. **Reward:** Explain the value the person receives from participating. This might include visibility for their work or expertise, learning opportunities or skill development, connection to community or influential people, compensation if other value isn't clear, or career advancement and portfolio building. Articulating the value proposition transforms your ask from extraction to exchange.

Understanding and implementing all three components ensures your requests create sustainable partnerships.

Critical Rule

Never thank preemptively. Saying "Thanks in advance" assumes they'll say yes and can quickly turn a positive transaction into a negative one. This seemingly polite phrase actually removes their agency and pressures them into compliance.

Reflection

The Three R's Model reveals that "transactional" shouldn't be a dirty word. Good relationships are built on fair transactions where everyone receives value. Bad relationships extract value from one party for another's benefit.

The recognition component often feels uncomfortable to people who don't want to seem overly flattering. But specific recognition isn't flattery—it's respect. You're showing that you've done your homework, that you understand their work, and that you're making a thoughtful request rather than spamming everyone.

The request component requires overcoming our tendency to be vague. We worry that too many details will seem demanding. But ambiguity creates anxiety and leads to declining offers. When people know exactly what's expected, they can make informed decisions. Specificity is respectful.

The reward component is where many asks fail. We assume the value is obvious ("It's exposure!") or we're uncomfortable being explicit about value exchange ("That feels mercenary"). But if you can't articulate why someone should say yes beyond "to help me," you probably shouldn't be asking. And "exposure" is only valuable if you can quantify it specifically.

The model works because it creates sustainable relationships. When both parties benefit from interactions, they're eager for future collaboration. When only one party benefits, goodwill depletes quickly. The difference between developers who become long-term partners and those who respond once and then disappear usually comes down to whether your asks follow the Three R's.

Money deserves special mention: If you're asking on behalf of a company and can't articulate non-monetary value, pay people. Developer advocates sometimes resist this because it feels like their relationships should be "above" payment. That's backwards. Payment is a form of respect, acknowledging that someone's time and expertise have value. If you want sustainable relationships with external developers, compensate them fairly for their contributions.

APPENDIX K

DX Audits

Model Overview

The DX Audits Model provides a structured framework for documenting, reporting, and addressing product friction. Audits transform abstract developer frustrations into concrete, actionable evidence that drives product improvements.

The goal is straightforward: experience a given developer's workflow, document findings thoroughly, and surface actionable steps to reduce friction. Each audit focuses on a single use case—essentially a workflow that a developer would complete to accomplish a specific task (e.g., "add monitoring to a GraphQL server" or "deploy a Slack app to production"). This focused approach ensures your findings are specific and actionable rather than vague and overwhelming.

Four-Step Process

The DX Audits Model follows a consistent progression through four distinct phases:

1. **Discover:** Gather context before experiencing the workflow.
2. **Build:** Complete the workflow while creating a friction log.
3. **Report:** Summarize findings and deliver to decision-makers.
4. **Follow Up:** Track action items to completion.

Each step builds on the previous one to create a complete picture from initial research through final implementation.

K. Kemple, *Effective DevRel*, https://doi.org/10.1007/979-8-8688-2373-2

Value Proposition

The structured audit process delivers several critical benefits:

- Makes abstract feedback concrete and actionable
- Creates a paper trail from audit to resulting changes
- Provides a consistent, repeatable process across team
- Builds credibility when advocating for developers

These benefits compound over time as you build a library of evidence-based recommendations.

Step 1: Discover (Before the Work)

Before diving into the workflow itself, gather context about the use case you're about to audit. Depending on what initiates the audit, you might already have enough context, or you might want more information.

Draw from both the community and customers through GitHub issues, forums, social media, events, surveys, support tickets, and customer success feedback. Also, gather stakeholder input from product updates, road maps, engineering timelines, and strategic priorities.

Why discovery matters: Your feedback is only as good as the context you have. Without understanding the full scope and having strong cross-functional relationships, your feedback won't be as impactful.

Discovery Checklist

Before beginning your audit, ensure you can check these boxes:

- Understand the complete workflow from start to finish.
- Know the target persona (who typically completes this workflow).
- Identify related documentation and resources.
- Review any existing feedback on this workflow.

- Confirm the use case aligns with strategic priorities.
- Ensure relevant stakeholders expect your feedback.

Completing this discovery phase sets the foundation for meaningful findings.

Step 2: Build (Experience the Workflow)

Work through the developer workflow and record your experience in a friction log. You'll typically build a project that allows you to experience the workflow you want to audit, though sometimes you'll work entirely within a product UI.

Best Practices

Five key principles guide effective friction logging:

1. **Channel your empathy:** Approach the workflow as a developer might. Make no assumptions and question if steps would be more difficult for someone without your insider knowledge.
2. **More detail is better than less:** Provide enough context that anyone can read the document and understand or retrace your steps to reach the same outcome.
3. **Don't forget the good:** Document delightful experiences and include positive steps in your summary. Understanding what works well is as important as identifying problems.
4. **Use a consistent format:** Everyone should use the same template for friction logs to maintain accessibility and structure.
5. **Include empathy:** Think about how far someone not paid to do this would go before giving up. No one likes delivering negative feedback, but if you get stuck or would quit the workflow if not paid to continue, mark it as high friction.

Following these principles ensures your friction logs are credible, actionable, and valuable to the teams who need to act on them.

Friction Log Template

To standardize friction logging across your team, implement a template that captures all essential elements using the stoplight framework. Here's a template you can adapt:

```
# Title

## Summary
A high level summary of the findings.

## Objective
What is the purpose of this friction log? What developer journey will you
try to complete?

## Persona
Who is the developer that is likely to go through this journey? A self-
serve developer? An enterprise developer?

## Environment
What was the environment you used to complete this journey?

## Insights
- What did you feel about the work overall? Did your hypothesis match the
  outcome? Was there anything unexpected?
- Did you have any realizations or discover anything new? What is your
  measured opinion about the journey?

## Legend
🟢 - No Friction (positive experience)
🟡 - Low Friction (would continue but not a positive experience)
🔴 - High Friction (would/could not continue, negative experience)

## Steps
1. 🟡 This is where you record the actual steps you took to complete the
      workflow.
2. 🟢 Make sure to include the level of friction you experienced for
      each step.
3. 🟡 Anyone reading this document should clearly understand the exact
      steps you took to complete the friction log.
4. 🟢 Be sure to include the positive steps as well!
```

```
5. ● Use empathy and think about how far someone not paid to do this
     would go.

## Possible Solutions
- Step 1: Capture possible solutions to the friction you encounter here.
- Step 2: These possible solutions are what become your Actionable
Feedback!

## References
- A list of JIRA tickets, Slack messages, external forum links, and
  conversations where there is extra context about the friction being
  experienced.
```

This stoplight framework provides immediate visual cues about the severity of friction at each step while ensuring consistency across friction logs, making them easier to analyze, compare, and act upon.

Step 3: Report (Summarize and Deliver)

Add an executive summary to the friction log that distills your findings into digestible insights. Include highlights of what worked well in the experience, lowlights showing significant friction points encountered, key insights capturing realizations or discoveries from completing the journey, and actionable steps providing specific recommendations for addressing friction.

Delivery considerations: Use best judgment about where and when to deliver feedback. For unexpected feedback contexts, ensure you include the right people and have the necessary buy-in. Deliver to decision-makers who can act on findings, and frame findings as opportunities for improvement, not criticism.

The way you present your findings can determine whether they're acted upon or ignored.

Step 4: Follow Up (Track to Completion)

Work on the action items outlined in the friction log and track progress on any items requiring cross-team collaboration. Get links to track progress of action items (JIRA issues, documents, etc.), connect audit directly to resulting work, ensure nothing falls through the cracks, and document outcomes in a central database.

Why follow-up matters: This step creates a direct paper trail from your work to resulting changes, demonstrating DevRel's impact on product improvements. Without follow-up, even the best audit loses its value.

Reflection

The DX Audits Model reveals that effective developer advocacy isn't about having opinions—it's about having evidence. Anyone can say "developers find this confusing." An advocate with a friction log can say, "here are the exact steps where developers get stuck, here's how long they struggle, here's what they try, and here's what would fix it."

The model works because it transforms subjective experience into objective documentation. When you bring friction logs to product meetings, you're not arguing based on intuition—you're showing exactly what happens when developers use your product. That evidence is hard to dismiss.

The follow-up step is what separates this from typical feedback processes. Most feedback gets logged and forgotten. By tracking action items to completion and documenting outcomes, you create proof of your impact. This is crucial for demonstrating DevRel's value and for personal career growth.

The biggest challenge is time. Thorough friction logs take hours or even days to complete properly. Many DevRel professionals skip audits because they feel too busy with "real work." This is backwards thinking. A single thorough friction log that drives meaningful product improvements delivers more value than dozens of reactive support responses or mediocre content pieces.

The model also requires humility. When you document every step honestly, including your struggles, you're admitting that your product isn't perfect. This vulnerability is actually an asset—it builds trust with product teams who appreciate honest assessment over cheerleading.

Start with high-impact workflows (onboarding, first deployment, common integration patterns). These audits deliver maximum value because friction in these areas affects large numbers of developers. As you build credibility with the process, you can expand to more specialized workflows.

Remember: Friction logs aren't about finding problems for the sake of criticism. They're about making your platform easier to use, which directly benefits both developers and your business. Every friction point removed is another reason for developers to choose and stick with your platform.

APPENDIX L

Pre-Content Checklist

Model Overview

The Pre-Content Checklist provides a five-part framework for scoping and planning content before creation begins. The approach recognizes that quality content depends more on preparation than inspiration—it's about doing the work before the work.

Creating content is like creating software. Without clear requirements and constraints, you can't assess completion properly and might not end up with a result that fits the need. This checklist ensures you have those requirements in place before you start creating.

Two-Part Structure

The checklist divides preparation into two distinct phases, each serving a specific purpose in the planning process:

1. **Content scoping:** Define what you're creating before you begin—your objective (why is this content needed?), motivation (what should readers do or take away?), and persona (who is this for?).

2. **Content discovery:** Create the actual framework for your content—your hook (compelling intro that grabs attention) and questions (what might readers ask?).

Together, these two parts provide the foundation for efficient, effective content creation.

K. Kemple, *Effective DevRel*, https://doi.org/10.1007/979-8-8688-2373-2

Part 1: Content Scoping

Before writing a single word, you need to define three fundamental elements that will guide every decision you make during creation.

Objective (The Goal)

Define why this content is needed. Every piece should attach to a clear goal. Examples include the following:

- Raise awareness of new product capabilities.
- Address a specific developer pain point.
- Share best practices for common scenarios.
- Respond to frequently asked questions.
- Fill gaps in developer workflows.

Ask yourself what problem this content solves, why this content is needed now, how this aligns with business objectives, and what happens if you don't create this content. These questions ensure your content serves a real purpose.

Motivation (The Call to Action)

Define what readers should walk away with or what action they should take. Examples include the following:

- Try a new feature that solves their problem.
- Sign up for an event or program.
- Build with best practices and share with others.
- Understand a concept they can apply to work.
- Make informed decisions about tools or approaches.

Consider what readers should do after consuming this content, what knowledge or capability they should gain, and how you'll know if the content succeeded. Clear motivation creates measurable success criteria.

Persona (The Audience)

Define who you're creating this for. This determines messaging approach, prerequisites needed, and what to explain vs. assume. Examples include

- Experienced Node.js developers
- Developers new to GraphQL
- Enterprise security decision-makers
- Frontend developers working with REST APIs
- Technical leaders evaluating platform options

Ask yourself what their experience level is, what they already know, what their goals and pain points are, what context they have, and what language or terminology resonates with them. Understanding your audience prevents creating content that's too basic or too advanced.

After completing content scoping, you should have a clear goal, a clear call to action, a clear audience, and a foundation for all creation decisions.

Part 2: Content Discovery

With your scope defined, you can now create the actual framework that will guide your content creation.

Hook (The Introduction)

Create a compelling intro that grabs attention, addresses initial skepticism, and clearly defines what the content covers. The hook must be relatable to your persona and set appropriate expectations.

Strong hooks share several characteristics:

- Opens with a relatable problem or question
- Creates curiosity about the solution
- Clearly states what content will deliver
- Sets appropriate tone for the audience
- Makes the reader want to continue

Develop your hook through an iterative process:

1. Write draft opening paragraph.
2. Share with others who match your persona.
3. Ask: "Does this resonate? What questions do you have?"
4. Refine based on feedback.
5. Test again until it consistently resonates.

This testing process ensures your hook connects with real readers before you invest time in full content creation.

Questions (The Outline)

Identify questions readers might have about your topic. These questions form the basis of your content outline.

Use multiple discovery methods to gather comprehensive questions:

- Share the hook with others and ask what questions they have.
- Research existing content on the topic and identify gaps.
- Check forums, GitHub, and support channels for community questions.
- Review related documentation for missing pieces.
- Consider natural progression of learning.
- Think about common misconceptions.

Transform questions into a structured outline:

1. List all relevant questions without filtering.
2. Group related questions into themes.
3. Order themes in logical progression.
4. Identify which questions must be answered vs. optional.
5. Create section headings from question groups.
6. Assign specific questions to each section.

After completing content discovery, you should have a compelling hook that resonates with your audience, a clear outline based on actual reader questions, and acceptance criteria for completion (all questions answered).

After Checklist Complete: Choose Medium

With your preparation complete, you can choose the most appropriate format based on your content's needs. Consider update frequency, specificity, and timeline when making this decision.

The most common content formats each serve distinct purposes:

1. **Blog post:** Best for content that may need updates, detailed technical explanations, SEO-valuable content, portable content that can be republished elsewhere, and long-term reference material. Blog posts offer permanence and searchability while remaining easy to update as information changes.
2. **Video:** Best for visual demonstrations, step-by-step tutorials, personality-driven content, content benefiting from seeing live interaction, and situations where video production infrastructure exists. Video excels at showing rather than telling, making it ideal for complex visual workflows.
3. **Talk/Presentation:** Best for live interaction with audience, conference or event requirements, content benefiting from Q&A, networking opportunities, and content that may evolve based on audience feedback. Presentations create immediate engagement and allow real-time adaptation to audience needs.

The right medium amplifies your message—choosing poorly can undermine even the best-prepared content, while choosing well multiplies its impact.

Reflection

The Pre-Content Checklist reveals that writer's block and content struggles usually stem from unclear requirements rather than lack of inspiration. When you sit down without knowing exactly who you're writing for, why, or what questions to answer, every sentence becomes a negotiation with yourself about direction.

The scoping section (Objective, Motivation, Persona) provides the constraints that make creation easier, not harder. When you know you're writing for "experienced Node.js developers who need to add monitoring" rather than "developers in general," every decision becomes clearer—what to explain, what to assume, what terminology to use, and what depth to go into.

The discovery section (Hook, Questions) front-loads the hard thinking that usually happens during creation. By testing your hook with real people and gathering actual questions, you're validating your approach before investing hours in creation. This prevents the painful experience of writing 2000 words only to realize they don't resonate with your audience.

The questions-to-outline approach is particularly powerful. Instead of trying to predict what should be in your content, you're responding to what actual readers want to know. This ensures relevance while providing a clear structure. When you can look at your outline and know exactly which questions each section answers, writing becomes about explanation rather than invention.

Index

A

B

C

K. Kemple, *Effective DevRel*, https://doi.org/10.1007/979-8-8688-2373-2

D

E

N

O

P

Q

R

S

T, U, V

W, X

Y, Z

GPSR Compliance

The European Union's (EU) General Product Safety Regulation (GPSR) is a set of rules that requires consumer products to be safe and our obligations to ensure this.

If you have any concerns about our products, you can contact us on ProductSafety@springernature.com

In case Publisher is established outside the EU, the EU authorized representative is:

Springer Nature Customer Service Center GmbH
Europaplatz 3
69115 Heidelberg, Germany

Batch number: 10135453

Printed by Printforce, the Netherlands